PELICAN BOOKS
A269
CHRISTIANITY
S. C. CARPENTER

CHRISTIANITY

S. C. CARPENTER, D.D.

Sometime Dean of Exeter

PENGUIN BOOKS

MELBOURNE · LONDON · BALTIMORE

Penguin Books Ltd, Harmondsworth, Middlesex

U.S.A. : Penguin Books Inc., 3300 Clipper Mill Road, Baltimore 11, Md
[*Educational Representative:*
D. C. Heath & Co, 285 Columbus Avenue, Boston 16, Mass.]

AUSTRALIA : Penguin Books Pty Ltd, 200 Normanby Road,
Melbourne, S.C.5, Victoria

AGENT IN CANADA: Riverside Books Ltd, 47 Green Street,
Saint Lambert, Montreal, P.Q.

—

Made and printed in Great Britain by
The Whitefriars Press Ltd, Tonbridge

—

First published 1953

CONTENTS

I

Where is Christianity to be found?

NEWMAN wrote in 1839 of what was then beginning to be
called the Oxford Movement that:

It is not here or there; it has no progress, no causes, no fortunes;
it is a Spirit afloat, neither in the secret chamber nor in the desert,
but everywhere. It is within us, rising up in the heart where it is
least expected, and working its way, though not in secret, yet so
subtly and impalpably, as hardly to admit of precaution or en-
counter or any ordinary human rules of opposition. It is an adversary in the air ... the result of causes far deeper than political or
other visible agencies, the spiritual awakening of spiritual wants.

There is a sense in which something like this is true of Christianity itself, though Newman would hardly have allowed
the assertion. For it is often found in unexpected places.
Again and again it is anonymous. It is at work in persons
who do not know the name of the thing that moves them.
Yet it does move them. Because of it they are different from
what they would be if it did not exist. W. H. Mallock in
The New Republic put into the mouth of the character representing Jowett of Balliol the remarkable statement that
'Christianity includes all religions, even any honest denial of
itself.' It is possible that Jowett, though he was said to have
been intensely exasperated by the portrait painted of him
under the name of Dr Jenkinson, would not altogether have
repudiated this particular utterance.

It is in fact much too sweeping. If it were to be accepted,
words would lose all meaning, and shadow would signify the
same as substance. More easy it is to appreciate the generous
obituary tribute of Andrew Lang to his agnostic friend
Grant Allen: 'A sad good Christian after all.' John Henry
Shorthouse, brought up among the Friends, and in later

life an Anglican whose admiration of seventeenth-century churchmanship did not prevent him from being of the Liberal School, believed that there were circumstances in which an agnostic could rightly present himself to receive Holy Communion. A like conviction, though it did not go so far, was expressed by Thomas Hardy.

These illustrations are all from past generations. It is to-day in one way harder, in another easier, to speak of Christianity as existing in this rather abstract and non-ecclesiastical, or at least extra-ecclesiastical, form. It is harder, because those Victorians who rejected the Christian dogma held fast to the Christian ethic and believed that it could stand alone. They were mistaken, though it was an error that did credit to their hearts. It cannot stand alone. It was never intended to. There are of course still plenty of unreflecting persons who suppose that a man who pays his bills and is kind-hearted may rightly be described as a good Christian, but those who definitely reject Christianity to-day often reject both dogma and ethic. Accordingly, for that reason there is, or at least it would seem probable that there would be, less of this rather disembodied Christianity than there was. The increased frankness of to-day helps us all to know more clearly where we are.

On the other hand it is easier, because something of the old idea of Christian Europe, or the Christian West, has risen again in recent years in Britain, in many parts of Europe, and no doubt, *mutatis mutandis*, in America and elsewhere. The emergence of black and evil forces, racial hatred, inordinate ideological and military ambition, political persecution, contempt for freedom, physical cruelty, a habit of deliberate and shameless lying in the conduct of political and diplomatic affairs, and the collapse in many quarters of the old generally accepted standards of honesty – all this has shocked a large number of decent people so gravely that the only name they can find for it is the spirit of Antichrist. The course of events has moved them to say: 'We are the inheritors of the old Christian tradition of Europe. We represent Christendom.' Mr Churchill speaks often of 'Christian civilization'. Mr Ernest Bevin, in the House of Commons, speaking of some course of action which he desired utterly to repudiate, said, 'It is against our religion.'

It is not only political. It is also intellectual. Certain of the *intelligentsia*, who formerly had a contempt for Christianity, are changing their opinion. What has happened is this. They used to assume that what was the matter with the world, that is, with people other than themselves, was ignorance. Let us have better education, they said, and it will be all right. Since then they have perceived what they did not know before, that evil is a real thing. It stalks, naked and menacing, through the world, seeking whom it may devour. This fact has caused many of the intellectuals to think more seriously and more respectfully of Christian doctrines. Yes, Christian doctrines. And, above all, the once rather specially obnoxious doctrine of Original Sin. Robert Browning in *Gold Hair* assigned to this doctrine a high place among the 'reasons and reasons' for believing Christianity to be true, but he did not convert the intellectuals either of his own or of the two following generations. Even the theologians were disposed to put the old doctrine forward rather apologetically. It is now perceived that this doctrine explains things, or, in the phrase of one cautious philosopher, 'reduces the inexplicability of things'. It explains why progress is so discontinuous, why there are so many setbacks. It teaches the lesson – and there are, after all, not a few examples in human history which suggest that it is true – which G. K. Chesterton expressed by saying that 'I must be prepared for the moral fall of any man from any position at any moment, and especially for my fall from my position at this moment.'

There is another quarter, no less intelligent, and for the most part, deeply interested in politics, but with a rather less specialized outlook, and perhaps rather less sense of imminent desperate conflict, where there exists a Christian tradition, where Christian sympathies prevail, where some degree of Christian practice is often observed. The ethos of it is not whole-heartedly orthodox, nor conspicuously devout. It is more than what the ladies of Erewhon rather optimistically expected would be forthcoming from their husbands if the Musical Banks were ever seriously attacked, but it is less than the minimum desired, and claimed, by any Church. It is the benevolent attitude of many in the Services, the Law, Medicine, and other professions, more than neutrality, less than enthusiasm. Among the black-coated, and occasionally, even now, silk-hatted men, who may be found on a Sunday morning in such places as the Temple Church or the other Inns of Court Chapels, or Westminster Abbey, there are some who are eager Christians. And there are some who are less sure, but feel that it is Christianity or nothing.

It would seem, then, that there is a good deal of rather fluid Christianity. Oscar Wilde at the end of his life, after he had passed through a terrible ordeal, wrote:

> How else but through a broken heart
> May Lord Christ enter in?

But long before that, while he was still a successful dilettante genius, he had written:

> And yet, and yet,
> These Christs that die upon the barricades,
> God knows it, I am with them – in some things.

Apart from barricades, which constitute a special case, there is much of this feeling in people to-day. There is more than that. Wilde's patronizing semi-approval, like A. H. Clough's combination of an eager wish that Christianity might be true and regretful inability to believe it, is perhaps too essentially of the nineteenth century to represent the mood of to-day. The mood, or at least a common mood, to-day is to claim what a distinguished Unitarian once called 'the much-loved Christian name'. The claim very often does not materialize into public adherence to the Christian Church or into devotion of the traditional kind. It may sometimes be no more than a feeling that there is Christ and there is Antichrist, and the right course for a decent man is to take his stand with Christ. At any rate the issue is sharper than it used to be.

It is of course important in the interests of truth not to overstate the case. Words are often used loosely. The man who is asked, 'Are you a Christian?' and replies, 'I hope so', betrays by his answer that he is not. For, if he were, he would know it. There are even those who describe themselves as 'Christians in the best sense of the word', meaning by that some private and probably very unsatisfactory sense of their own. Our Lord said, 'He who is not against us is with us', but, moving nearer to the centre, He also said, 'He who is not for me is against me.'

There is a famous scene in the Book of Joshua. Joshua, leader of the Israelites in their attempt to win the Promised Land, saw one standing over against him 'with his sword drawn in his hand'. And Joshua went unto him, and said unto him, 'Art thou for us, or for our adversaries?' And he said, 'Nay, but as Captain of the hosts of the Lord am I now come.' And Joshua fell on his face to the earth, and did worship, and said unto him, 'What saith my Lord unto his servant?'

To pretend that this represents exactly the response of all or even most modern people to religious influences would be, for the present writer or his like, wishful thinking. It is not yet anything like that. But it may be said that there is present to the eyes of very many the dim outline of a Figure. The weapon in his hand is not precisely a sword, though it is sword-shaped. It is in fact cross-handled. But it is not a weapon of material destruction. It is a symbol of another kind of warfare, for the casting down of strongholds, a warfare 'not against flesh and blood, but against principalities, against powers, against the rulers of the darkness of this world, against spiritual wickedness in high places.' Joshua's words, 'What saith my Lord unto his servant?'

have not yet been spoken, but it is possible that something like them may be heard before very long.

All this is rather at the higher cultural level. At the more densely-populated level where men and women have had only an elementary education and have not, as some have, to their enormous credit, supplemented it for themselves in after years, there is a great mass of indifference, and some hostility. This mass is nevertheless aware of Christianity. It is apt to make cynical references to the difference between Christians and Christ. These are often no more than self-excusing debating points, but they show that the indifference is not quite total. The general attitude might fairly be called good-natured. Even the hostility is sometimes pierced by a misgiving which recalls that Saul of Tarsus was said to have kicked against the goad. There is a story in *France Alive* of two men who during the German occupation had worked in the same gang and had become friends. One was a Christian, the other an atheistic Communist. The Christian was being led off to some punishment. His friend whispered to him, 'I'll pray for you.' Afterwards the Christian said, 'Why did you say that? You don't believe in it.' The other replied, 'It was all that I could do, and I thought you would like it.' Misery acquaints a man with strange bed-fellows, and perhaps this exact thing would not happen very often in the less stimulating post-war period. Perhaps the utmost that could be said is that in England the indifference is mainly good-natured, and the hostility is hardly ever savage.

Thus it would seem that there is a certain diffused Christianity, a certain belief in Christian standards. But, whatever there is, it does not exist in its own right. It is either a survival, or something else. What else? 'Parasite' is an unpleasant term. Is 'Passenger' any better? 'Associate' is perhaps more complimentary. At all events, there is in the idea of it some notion of association with, or derivation from, some original parental force. The diffused form of Christianity is only possible because there is a central core of life and fire. If there are anywhere appendages, or extensions, or maybe augmentations, there must be that to which they are attached. As Dr H. L. Goudge shrewdly said of the Old Testament, 'Had there been no prophecy, we should not care to read the story of Israel. Had there been no priesthood, there would be no story to read.'

Some of the old champions of Christianity in the Latin-speaking West were not very attractive characters. Tertullian, the African zealot, was hard and intolerant, and even Cyprian of Carthage, smoother and more courteous, was too much of the ecclesiastic to suit all tastes. Much more attractive than Tertullian is his Greek-speaking contemporary, Clement of Alexandria, a modern among the ancients, liberal, eager to use pagan learning in the service of Christian faith, a Christian Platonist, almost a Christian Gnostic. Yet it is the Tertullians rather than the Clements who have saved Christianity from dissolution. The loosening of what may have been over-rigid definitions, with occasional excursions into the No Man's Land that lies beyond the known Christian territory, and the noting of bits of Aeschylus or Plato, of Virgil or Seneca, or, in our own time, of Whitehead or Aldous Huxley, which seem to have a Christian ring, all this is interesting, and may commend the cause to the hard of hearing, but what St Paul calls the defence and confirmation of the Gospel is mostly done by those of tougher quality. In any case, the contrast is not wholly between Greek and Latin. The Greek Orthodox Churches of the East have always been careful guardians of the Faith.

There must be thinkers, whether they be Greek, Latin, or modern, of the more institutional and more severely theological type. Even if the old comparison of the Christian Church with an ark, a safe refuge amid the stormy and dangerous waters of a flood, be laid aside as too rigid and departmental, there is still the comparison with a fire, which has its essential core of heat, and also warms the air all round. Because theologians have battled for the indispensable *credenda*, and saints have knelt on bare stone floors, there can be a diffused glow on the circumference of a large circle. Spirit, as William Temple used to say, always clothes itself in body. The body at any given time may be plain, or even ugly, because the human elements of which it is composed are poor things, but the spirit must have a home somewhere. Therefore a volume which bears, however inadequately, the title of 'Christianity', must not be content to range about the boundaries of a more or less Christian region. It must describe the central citadel, and it must give some account of how the citadel came to be what it is. Accordingly, the chapters which follow will be largely, though not wholly, concerned with Christianity in its more institutional aspect. And they will begin with an historical enquiry into the nature of the seed-plot in which Christianity arose.

2

The Antecedents of Christianity

THE author of Ecclesiastes was no doubt unduly pessimistic when he said that there was no new thing under the sun, but it is quite true that many things are less new than is commonly supposed. They may seem to be beginning now, but they really began a long time ago. Most of all is this true of large stirrings of the human spirit. It is true of Christianity.

Christianity may with perfect accuracy be said to have begun with the advent of Jesus Christ, but it is also true that He entered a world which was prepared for His coming. Not in the sense that the people of the world, even those of His own race and nation, were ready for Him or accepted Him at once, or indeed that anyone then living knew that the world was so prepared. God always has much in His Purpose which was unexpected by men at the time of its occurrence, but discerning men can see afterwards that God was moving on regular, patient and consistent lines.

The world was prepared, as St Paul presently perceived, and as we can all see now quite easily, in the sense that the hand of God had planted in the human mind longings, in a greater or less degree articulate, which Christ could and did satisfy. The purpose of God had so ruled history that there was one Empire and one speech throughout the Mediterranean world. The Spirit of God had so illuminated the minds of very many among the pagans that they had begun to see the futility of the old cults, and so were ripe for a new and more spiritual faith. And, finally, God had so cultivated the soil in one quarter of the world that seed sown in it would, at least here and there, take root and grow.

The old questioning of the justice of a 'chosen race',

summed up in the jesting words 'How odd of God, to choose the Jews!' has rather lost its savour, since Armitage Robinson pointed out that 'selection' rather than 'election' was the true rendering of the word by which St Paul described the divine purpose for Israel. They were not 'favourites'. They were the material for an experiment. A divine revelation, if the possibility of such a thing be conceded, must be planted somewhere. Even if it be for the moment concentrated in the person of one man, say Abraham, or Moses, the man is surrounded by a family, a community, a nation, or the makings of a nation. If, further, it has, as any revelation or ideal of an ethical character must have, social implications, it spreads out into a way of life lived, or aimed at, by a number of people.

The governing fact about the origins of Christianity is that it was born and grew up on Jewish soil. It spoke the Jew's language and it thought the Jew's thoughts. The New Testament is unanimous about this. The Third Gospel and the Acts, the two books which certainly came from a Gentile pen, understand it perfectly. You can see that the author is a Gentile, but he does justice to the Semitic setting in the whole of his first book, and in the first half of the second, with the imaginative skill of a real historian. Even the Fourth Gospel, which is, whoever the author, very fully emancipated from the early Semitic limitations, although it has some anachronisms and the hostile 'Jews' are perhaps those of the writer's own period, when the breach has been widening and hardening for sixty years, rather than of the Master's own earthly life, is full of minute and accurate evidence of faithfulness to the historical setting. The author even here and there corrects some detail in the Synoptic narrative, as, for example, the date of the Last Supper, where it seemed to him that a mistake had been made. Browning makes St John say:

> Patient, I stated much of the Lord's life,
> Forgotten or misdelivered, and let it work.

And, though his book is an interpretation, and therefore super-historical, it is not un-historical. Thus, even where the difference between the old and the new is most clearly seen, there is continuity. To turn the page which divides the first part of the Bible from the second leads into a new world, but not an alien world.

The original disciples of Jesus were all Jews. And if it be suggested that, with the exception of Judas, they all seem to have come from Galilee, the most Hellenized region of the Holy Land, they were not of the sort with whom the process of Hellenization could have gone appreciably far. They were all Jews, and it was the first major problem of the infant Church to determine whether Gentile converts were to be accepted, and, if so, on what terms. Just at the very first there were no Gentile converts. The early chapters of Acts reveal a community of disciples of Jesus, born Jews, who continued to live and worship in the traditional Jewish way, adding to their old faith a belief in the Resurrection and Messiahship of Jesus, and to their old practice the initiatory rite of Baptism and the weekly, perhaps daily, rite of the Breaking of the Bread. St Peter thinks it quite natural to go up to the Temple at the hour of prayer, and it is even recorded at one period that a great company of priests was obedient to the faith. They were at first a sort of Guild within the Jewish Church.

The religion of the Jew can in fundamentals be discovered from the Old Testament, though by the beginning of the Christian era the original scriptures had been supplemented by a large body of tradition, to which, in matters of conduct, much importance was attached.

There was a time in our own history when the Old Testament, except for the ceremonial law, which was never held to be binding, was regarded by many Christian people as of primary authority. It was part of the Bible, and that was that. Although even the seventeenth-century Puritans would no doubt have agreed, if challenged, that the Christian Scriptures had the greater authority, yet much in the

Old Testament which had been actually superseded or even deliberately corrected in the later volume, was accepted and defended as 'in the Bible', and used freely as a sanction. Because Samuel had hewed Agag in pieces before the Lord, therefore it was permissible to execute King Charles. In that century and long after, because the Israelites had been bidden to do no work on the seventh day of the week, it was thought wrong to sew on a button or to play a game on the first.

During the nineteenth century critical methods of interpretation came into use, and there were not a few who passed to the other extreme. The Old Testament was often thought of as a mass of legends, a store-house of interesting material for the study of Hebrew religion, and not very much more. A truer view has emerged lately. Critical in assigning dates and distinguishing varieties of authorship, and never expecting to find Christian heads on Old Testament shoulders, it recognizes in the Old Testament the first half of the book of true religion, the story of the education, up to the time of their great testing, of the People of God. The *Dramatis Persona* of the Old Testament is God, and the plot from beginning to end is the unfolding of the divine purpose. It was the constant theme of St Paul that this purpose had never been understood, had in fact never been clearly disclosed, until it was realized in Christ. This is 'the mystery', once hidden, now revealed, of which he speaks in the Epistles to the Romans and Ephesians.

The Christian disciples of the first generation inherited, unhesitatingly and enthusiastically, the great and splendid things for which Israel had stood. Chief among these was the ethical monotheism of the Old Testament. There are scholars of eminence who consider that Moses was a monotheist, but the common opinion is that the position was only gradually reached. In early days Jehovah was their God, and it was freely conceded that Milcom was the god of the Ammonites and Chemosh of the Moabites. Jehovah was of course better and more powerful than the other gods, and in point of fact there was always a strong ethical element in the Jehovah-cult which made it different from the religions of other nations. But it was not at first Monotheism. It could be called Henotheism, or Monolatry. Moreover, even so, there were in early days constant lapses, and the Book of Deuteronomy has severe warnings against whoring after strange gods. Gradually, the hands of the Divine Educator, by prophetic teaching and by the hard discipline of exile in Babylon, taught the Jews their lesson. Long before the Christian era the mind, will, and conscience of the Jew had come to be devoted to the one living and true God, Maker of Heaven and earth, Ruler of the Universe, controlling all Nature and all nations of the world. Idolatry, the worship of the creature instead of the Creator, was utterly abhorrent.

This faith had been proclaimed by the eighth-century prophets, and in even grander and more absolute terms by the sixth-century prophet who wrote Isaiah xl–lxvi. There is no finer statement in all literature of the divine Transcendence than:

To whom then will ye liken God? or what likeness will ye compare unto him?

Have ye not known? have ye not heard? hath it not been told you from the beginning? have ye not understood from the foundations of the earth?

It is he that sitteth upon the circles of the earth, and the inhabitants thereof are as grasshoppers; that stretcheth out the heavens as a curtain, and spreadeth them out as a tent to dwell in:

That bringeth the prisoners to nothing; he maketh the judges of the earth as vanity.

Yea, they shall not be planted; yea, they shall not be sown: yea, their stock shall not take root in the earth: and he shall also blow upon them, and they shall wither, and the whirlwind shall take them away as stubble.

To whom then will ye liken me, or shall I be equal? saith the Holy One.

Lift up your eyes on high, and behold who hath created these things, that bringeth out their host by number: he calleth them all by names by the greatness of his might, for that he is strong in power, not one faileth.

Hast thou not known? hast thou not heard, that the everlasting God, the Lord, the Creator of the ends of the earth, fainteth not, neither is weary? there is no searching of his understanding.

He giveth powers to the faint; and to them that have no might he increaseth strength.

Even the youths shall faint and be weary, and the young men shall utterly fall.

But they that wait upon the Lord shall renew their strength; they shall mount up with wings as eagles; they shall run, and not be weary; and they shall walk, and not faint.

(Isa. xl. 18, 21–26, 28–31.)

All this wealth of affirmation became at once the property of the Christians. That is why their earliest Creed-form was 'Jesus is Lord'. There was no need to teach Jewish converts to say, 'I believe in God the Father Almighty, Maker of Heaven and Earth.' The new thing was belief in Jesus.

In the Old Testament the affirmation had been backed by the story of the Israelite people. Asked by some questioner, 'Why do you speak of God as King, or Saviour, or Father?' any Jew would have replied at once, 'Because He has ruled us, and saved us, and been a Father to us.' The Old Testament constantly appeals to the Exodus, which had made Israel a nation, and to the Law, which gave them their way of life. Old Testament religion was a historical religion, not as Christianity is a historical religion, founded on certain facts in the earthly life of God Incarnate, but depending on what God had done for them as a nation. All this the Church took over.

The assumption was not made without protest from the Jew. The Christian claimed that the Old Testament promises had been inherited by the Church. The Christian Church was the new Israel. St Peter uses a whole chain of Old Testament phrases – 'a chosen generation, a royal priesthood, a holy nation, a peculiar people', as a description of the Christian Church. The anonymous author of the Epistle to the Hebrews sets himself to demonstrate that the

Great High Priest, the Ascended Christ, by His one Sacrifice, once made upon the Cross, and thereafter perpetually presented before the Father in Heaven, had accomplished all that the Levitical priests, with their continually repeated sacrifices, had vainly sought to do. St Paul, while never laying aside his 'heart's desire and prayer to God for Israel, that they might be saved,' was audacious in claiming that the Church was the true inheritor of the promises. Indeed, he must have greatly exasperated the Jews by the vehemence of his language, and by the illustrations which he chose. The Jews had always thought of themselves as children of Abraham through Isaac, and of Abraham's other son, Ishmael, as the ancestor of the Arabian tribes, not hostile, not hated, but foreigners. St Paul in Galatians iv audaciously asserts that Ishmael, 'the son born after the flesh', is the type of Israel, 'but we, brethren, as Isaac was, are the children of promise'. It was a hard saying. What Jew could hear it with equanimity? The Jew was accustomed to say in his devotions:

Thou hast brought a vine out of Egypt; thou hast cast out the heathen and planted it.

Thou madest room for it: and when it had taken root it filled the land.

The hills were covered with the shadow of it: and the boughs thereof were like the goodly cedar-trees.

She stretched out her branches unto the sea; and her boughs unto the river.   (Psalm lxxx, 8–11.)

He had gone on to say, when things were difficult, as they often were:

Why hast thou then broken down her hedge: that all they that go by pluck off her grapes?

But this was worse. This was the appropriation by these upstart and heretical Nazarenes of his own ancient vineyard, with himself apparently reduced to the position of an outsider.

A third element of the Old Testament religion which was

taken over by the Christian Church was belief in Messiah. The Jew had always looked forward to a Day of the Lord. Dr Inge once remarked that the Greek thought of himself as separated from Paradise by space. The Garden of the Hesperides was in the far West, beyond the Pillars of Hercules, in the land of the setting sun. To the Jew the interval was one of time. The Day of the Lord, which would usher in the millennium, was for him in the future. It would materialize, he believed, with the Advent of Messiah, the Anointed, in Greek *Christos*. There were various conceptions of Messiah, but what Meredith called the rapture of the forward view is thoroughly characteristic of the Old Testament. Perhaps the most common expectation was that of the Davidic King, who would be a great and powerful monarch:

His dominion shall be also from the one sea to the other: and from the flood unto the world's end.

They that dwell in the wilderness shall kneel before him: his enemies shall lick the dust.

The kings of Tharsis and of the isles shall give presents: the kings of Arabia and Saba shall bring gifts.

All kings shall fall down before him: all nations shall do him service.   (Psalm lxxii, 8–11.)

Above all, he would reign in righteousness:

For he shall deliver the poor when he crieth: the needy also, and him that hath no helper.

He shall be favourable to the simple and needy: and shall preserve the souls of the poor.

He shall deliver their souls from falsehood and wrong: and dear shall their blood be in his sight.

There were other pictures, the 'lowly king', riding upon an ass, there was the 'Suffering Servant', a picture which, if not precisely Messianic, is at all events that of a Saviour of the nation, and there is, especially at the end of the period, the apocalyptic picture of the Son of Man, who will come in glory to judge the world. In the post-Canonical book, the Similitudes of Enoch, the Son of Man is a superhuman figure, riding on the clouds of heaven, who will judge mankind and inaugurate the New Age.

The natural temptation of those nurtured on such hopes was to assume that the heathen peoples would be judged and condemned, and that they themselves would enter upon a period of prosperity, and even of world-leadership. The Prophet Amos had felt constrained to shatter these political, materialistic expectations. 'Woe unto you,' he cries, 'who desire the day of the Lord. To what end is it for you? The Day of the Lord is darkness, and not light.' The Prophets sought continually to break the pride of their fellow-countrymen, but they cannot be said to have succeeded. When the time was actually fulfilled for Messiah to appear there were here and there groups of pious people, like those described in the first two chapters of St Luke's Gospel, who 'looked for the redemption of Israel' with a desire that was predominantly spiritual, but the majority had other hopes. They were under the heel of the Roman conqueror, and though the title Zealot seems to have come in a little later than the date of the Nativity, there were plenty who looked for a Messiah who would unfurl the banner of revolt and raise the cry of 'Judaea for the Jews' and 'Down with Rome!' To put Himself at the head of such a movement was no doubt one of the possibilities which Jesus faced at His temptation in the wilderness. It would seem that these ideas were entertained by the rank and file rather than by the leaders of Judaism. The Pharisees had their ambitions, but they were more ecclesiastical than nationalist. The Sadducees had laid aside political ambition, and had made terms with the world and the Roman Empire. They were not looking for Messiah. Yet in the main the expectation, in one form or other, was very strong.

This Messianic expectation was taken over by the Christians, not merely as a hope but as an accomplished fact. They claimed that the hope had been realized among themselves. An expression that occurs occasionally in the Acts, 'proving from the Scriptures that Jesus was the Christ', would perhaps more accurately be rendered 'proving that the Christ was Jesus', i.e. that the expectation had been fulfilled in the person of Jesus. The Confession of Peter at Caesarea Philippi, 'Thou art the Christ', was the first time when any of the disciples of Jesus penetrated what has been called the 'Messianic secret'. It would seem that the Lord Himself had always felt Messiahship to be at least a part of His vocation, but He had not proclaimed it. Peter is even now instructed to tell no man, and in fact the secret was not made public until the occasion which we now know as Palm Sunday. The triumphal entry of that day into Jerusalem, modest and peaceful as it was, with the Master mounted, not on a war-horse, but on the domestic ass, was a proclamation of Messiahship, and it helped to turn the scale in the determination of the authorities that 'it was expedient that one man should die for the people'.

Messiah is a Hebrew word, an Old Testament word, a national word. It does not represent the whole of what Christians believe about Christ. But it was for Peter at Caesarea Philippi and for the man in the street on Palm Sunday, the highest category within reach.

The claim that the Messiah was Jesus was fiercely resisted by the Jews, both during what we call Holy Week and after. Our Lord during His ministry had many a clash with the Jewish ecclesiastical authorities. And the final clash ended, as it seemed, in their favour. From that time the idea of a crucified Messiah seemed an insult to their national pride, an insuperable stumbling-block. To Saul of Tarsus, in his persecuting days, Jesus was a shabby impostor, unorthodox, a Sabbath-breaker, consorting with the riff-raff of the nation, who had finally failed ignominiously and had suffered a felon's death on the traditionally accursed gallows. To talk of the resurrection of such an one from the dead was a manifest absurdity. The paradox, in which Saul of Tarsus presently learned to triumph and exult, had been very hard even for the Twelve to accept at their first hearing of it. The confession of Peter was followed immediately by the Lord's first announcement of His coming suffering and death, and when Peter, with the glow of his recent high moment still upon him, ventured to deprecate such talk, he received one of the sternest rebukes recorded in the Gospels.

There is much more in Christianity which came to it from the Old Testament, the thought of God as concerned simultaneously with the history of nations and the salvation of individual souls, as powerful and yet loving and compassionate, belief in the indissoluble connexion of ethics, especially sex-ethics, with religion, the touch of Puritanism, but all this will appear later when the content of the Christian Creed and Ethic falls to be examined. It is time to turn to other lines, less clearly marked, of what may be called the collateral descent of Christianity from other forbears.

With the very ancient civilizations Christianity has only indirect connexion. Crete, Babylon, and Egypt had all made their mark on Old Testament culture, and Christianity accordingly inherited, as part of its birthright, something that had come from those quarters. But the impression made by Crete through the Philistines, by Babylon through the Code of Hammurabi and an ancient cosmogony and some other early traditions, or by Egypt during a long and laborious apprenticeship to nationhood spent in that country, all that had become by the beginning of the Christian era very diffused, and was only inherited by Christianity in a very general way.

With Greece the case is very different. Hellenic influence was brought to bear upon pre-Christian Judaism, though it was not received very easily. The Jews were of all nations the most nationalist. They believed in keeping themselves to themselves, and preserving what they called the holy seed, but even they could not remain wholly unaffected by Hellenism. The Greeks and the Hebrews were both peoples with strongly marked characteristics, and ever since the time when they first began to clash Hebraism and Hellenism have everywhere been two contrasted types of

humanity. They are the two views of life which not only
produced Elijah and Plato, but among ourselves have
produced on the one hand Oliver Cromwell and Thomas
Carlyle and on the other hand Shakespeare, in one half of
his versatile personality, and, even more definitely, Keats.
They were at the time with which we are concerned very
different. Yet they had their contacts and infiltrations.
These began in the fourth century B.C.

When Alexander overran most of the known world, he
carried Greek culture with him. The city of Alexandria,
founded by him in 332 B.C., became a great centre of
Greek learning, and that was where the Jews first tasted
Hellenism. Many Jews lived at Alexandria, and the Sep-
tuagint, the famous Greek version of the Old Testament,
made there in the third and second centuries, had the effect
of introducing the Hebrew Scriptures to Greek-speaking
peoples. The Jews in the main resisted Hellenism. Those of
the Dispersion conceived it to be their duty to commend
their own ethical monotheism to the people among whom
they lived, and they had considerable success, but they
spoke the Greek language, and ideas are infectious.

The essential types had little in common. The devotion
of the Jews to the faith of their fathers, their family life,
their suspicion of most forms of art, on the ground that they
were inseparable from idolatry, and of the Greek Games as
likely to lead to sexual licence, made it impossible for
them to adopt Hellenism as a way of life. The Hellenists on
the other hand despised the Jews as uncultured and
narrow-minded. 'Hellenism protested against the narrow-
ness, barrenness, and intolerance of Judaism; Judaism
protested against the godlessness and immorality of Hellenism. Both were right in their protests, and yet each in a
sense needed the other.' [1]

The Palestinian Jews in particular put up a strong resis-
tance to the Hellenizing process, above all in the second
century B.C. when their Greek overlord, Antiochus

1. C. F. Kent, *The Makers and Teachers of Judaism*, 191.

Epiphanes, attempted to force it upon them. This led to the Maccabaean revolt, which, if ever a war can be so described, was a holy war. They were fighting for their altar, which Antiochus had desecrated. The story of this is told in the first Book of Maccabees, and can be read between the lines in the Book of Daniel. The campaign and what followed stamped upon the Palestinian Jews a more national character than ever.

Meantime, in the Dispersion, among Jews in Egypt and in Asia beyond Palestine, the Hellenistic influence was considerable. The Jews did not change their Creed nor their way of life, but they imbibed some Greek ideas. During what is called the Greek period the Hellenic influence operated in various ways. The Book of Jonah shows a wide and tolerant outlook which was not characteristic of Judaism. The author of Ecclesiastes learned his pessimism from Hellenic rather than Jewish sources. The Book of Wisdom, which probably came from Alexandria, is full of Greek influence. A little later, Philo, a learned Jew of Alexandria, set himself to reconcile the two cultures. Like many enthusiasts, he over-shot the mark. He tried to prove that Moses had been a kind of Hebrew Plato and Plato a kind of Attic Moses. At the same time there were non-Jewish writers, e.g. those called Hermetic, who from the other end were glad to claim the sanction of the Hebrew scriptures for their own mystical philosophy. Thus, among the Jews of the Dispersion, especially at Alexandria, the process of assimilation went a long way, and even from Palestine itself could not wholly be excluded.

Accordingly, when Christianity broke away from its parent Judaism, the parent was already to a certain extent Hellenized. The earliest Christians, though of Jewish race, were for the most part bilingual, and very soon there was a great influx of Asiatic and European Greeks, who were so numerous that they determined the future language of the Church, and imparted not a little of the colour of its thought. It must be enough to say about this colouring

27

that it was not nearly so great as has occasionally been maintained. What was contributed was not a transformation of an originally simple Semitic piety into a Greek mystery-religion, but a philosophic analysis of what had always been and continued to be a fundamentally Semitic theology.

The influence of Rome was felt in a quite different way. The consideration of it does not strictly belong to this context. The mention of it is an anachronism, but one hard to avoid. It did not come through Judaism. Though Judas Maccabaeus made a treaty with Rome, and though Syria, including Judaea became a Roman province in 63 B.C., Jews and Romans were poles apart. It was believed that Pompey had forced his way into the Holy of Holies, an unspeakable outrage, and there is an allusion in St Luke's Gospel to the Galileans whose blood Pilate had mingled with their sacrifices. There was no assimilation, or, if there was, it was the other way. It was the general Roman policy to be tolerant of local or national religions. It was a Roman habit to pick up some of the culture of the nations whom they had conquered. Disillusioned patricians, weary of their own cults, were looking round for new religions. There were some which came from Egypt and Phrygia, mysteries, with elaborate ceremonies and a promise of eternal life, and they had an appeal, but most of them were condemned by old-fashioned Romans as unwholesome. There was some interest in Judaism, an ancient, virile faith, with interesting holy books. Drusilla, wife of Felix the Governor before whom St Paul appeared, was a Jewess, as was Poppaea, Nero's mistress. The Herods cultivated friendly relations with Rome. The high priests accepted the Empire, and for their own sake made the best of it. In this way, while on the whole the Jews hated the Romans and the Romans despised the Jews, it may be said that Judaism made some impression on Roman life. Rome made none on Judaism. Even the cynical Sadducees, while they accepted Rome, had no intention of assimilating it.

Roman influence on Christianity came later, and in a much more direct way. There is little sign of it in the New Testament. The Empire was acknowledged as a fact, and there is no thought of rebellion. Our Lord in the wilderness refused the offer of the kingdoms of this world and the glory of them, and later said, 'Render unto Caesar the things that are Caesar's', though the conclusion of the sentence saves the injunction from any trace of what was later called Erastianism. St Paul and St Peter both enjoin obedience to the civil powers, and St Paul, writing under Nero (if 1 Timothy be really from his pen) directs that prayers, intercessions, and even thanksgivings be made for kings and all in authority. The only exception to this is in the Apocalypse, where Rome is the harlot, sitting upon seven hills, drunken with the blood of the saints, and even here it is noteworthy that the vengeance which the Seer expects to fall upon the City is from the hand of God, not man.

The Roman influence may be said in a way to have begun with St Paul. He was by patrimony a citizen of the Empire, and he occasionally used his citizenship to procure freedom to pursue his work. It may be supposed that he had felt something of the fascination of the ancient, famous capital, and it is certain that he had always longed 'to see Rome'. This would not be from any desire to observe the splendour of its buildings, or to indulge any secular civic pride, but for the sake of the Gospel. St Luke, with a strong sense of the dramatic, ends his second book with the arrival of the Apostle in the Imperial City, a prisoner indeed, but with liberty to say what he would to all who came to him. From the hour of his *Caesarem appello*, Christianity was bound up with the Empire. It could never escape. It never did. It grew up on the framework of the Empire, and, when the Empire fell, the Church succeeded and superseded it. There are those who think that St Paul foresaw something like that, and was, in a sense, a Christian Imperialist. It is at all events significant that his Epistle to

CHRISTIANITY

the Ephesians, in which he has much to say about the Body
of Christ, the Catholic Church, was written from Rome.

Even if St Paul may be said to have begun it, most of the
Roman influence came much later. As a Latin-speaking
and Latin-thinking Church gradually grew up in the West
(and in the early centuries an important part of it was in
North Africa), Latin ideas came more and more to be part
of Christian thought. The West was never so theological as
the East. The simple, straightforward Apostles' Creed is a
characteristic Western document. The Nicene Creed,
with its Platonic analysis, its substance-category and its
careful definitions, is characteristic of the East. The four
great Doctors of the West were all ecclesiastics. They were
competent theologians as well, but the contribution of the
West to Christianity was the maintaining of the solid fabric
of the Faith and the building of the solid fabric of the
Church. The old Romans had had a gift for law and order
and efficiency. They were hard men, but their machine
worked well, and the proof of that was that for a long time
wicked or ineffectual Emperors could not do much
damage to the machine. The Latin part of the Church
inherited this capacity. Augustine, living at a time when
the Empire was tottering to its fall, painted his famous
picture of the two Cities, the City of the world and the
City of God. Augustine had an immense influence on the
thought of later generations.

Thus rigid ideas of the Latin type came into Christianity – 'No salvation (or safety) outside the Church'; 'I
should not believe the Gospel if I were not moved by the
authority of the Catholic Church'; 'The Catholic Faith,
which except a man believe faithfully, he cannot be saved.'
The last one comes out of a period when the barbarians,
wild, lawless men, were beginning to be Christians. Their
mouths needed to be held with bit and bridle. Hence the
precision and severity of the document called *Quicunque
Vult*.

The convenience of setting the influence of Rome side

by side with that of Greece has led us far into Christian history. It is strange, and perhaps indefensible, that a chapter on the antecedents of Christianity should end with an allusion to a document of the fifth century A.D. But the tendencies which made Latin Christianity were nascent centuries before in the characters of Regulus, of the mother of the Gracchi, and of the elder Cato. The old motto *Roma semper eadem* is true in an even larger sense than that commonly assigned to it.

3

The Nativity of Christianity

IT would seem the natural thing to begin the actual story of the Christian religion with the Birth or at least with the beginning of the public ministry of Christ. It is not, however, illegitimate, and it may be profitable, to look ahead a few years, and catch sight of a cross-section.

The opening words of one of the earliest Christian documents, that called the First Epistle to the Thessalonians, are:

Paul, and Silvanus, and Timotheus, unto the Church of the Thessalonians which is in God the Father and in the Lord Jesus Christ: Grace be unto you, and peace, from God our Father, and the Lord Jesus Christ.

Let us suppose for a moment that all early Christian literature, except this simple sentence, has perished. There are no Gospels, no Acts, no Epistles, only these few dozen words. All we know about them is that they are the words of one Paulus, a travelling evangelist, of Jewish birth and training, who had founded some religious communities in Macedonia and elsewhere, and to one of them he had addressed the document of which these words are part. From this evidence, slight as it is in quantity, a good deal could be learned about the nature of early Christianity.

To begin with, the writer is a Jew. The Jews were a people with a passionate devotion to monotheism, and a passionate hatred of any kind of idolatry. The idea of rendering to any creature the worship due only to the Creator was utterly abhorrent to them. And yet this Jewish writer is here found speaking in the same breath of 'God the Father' *and* of another 'Name' (to avoid for the present question-begging terms), 'the Lord Jesus Christ'. Clearly something of great

32

moment has occurred to make this writer write like this. 'The Lord Jesus Christ' has made a profound, a revolutionary impression on the mind and conscience of the Jewish believer.

The remainder of this document, supposed just now for a special purpose to have perished, but actually in existence, is largely concerned with the expectation that this 'Lord Jesus Christ' would shortly return in glory, and consummate the Kingdom or Reign of God. It was an expectation which loomed large in primitive Christianity, and there are even some who suggest that primitive Christianity consisted of that and little more. It afterwards receded, partly because the expected event did not happen, but mainly because disciples came to understand more fully the whole of the Lord's teaching. In particular it was because they came to believe that the Promise – or at any rate a substantial instalment of it – had been realized in that Return of Christ in the Spirit, which had come to pass on the Day of Pentecost and had ever since provided the continual atmosphere of their religious life. They lived, as they said, 'in Christ', or 'in the Spirit'. The two expressions had the same value. They learned from Paul and even more from John that the state which they called the Kingdom of God and Eternal Life, while not perfectly accomplished in this life and therefore in a sense still future, was also a present reality. It is broadly true that the Kingdom of God seems in the Synoptic Gospels to be mainly a future thing, in St John mainly present, a thing which can be here and now. St Paul's eyes at first were fixed, not wholly but to a considerable extent, on the future, but he also taught and soon came to teach more and more a permanent Christ-mysticism. Dr Schweitzer allows that this is so, but he insists on calling this an apocalyptic mysticism, and in so doing, he radically modifies his original contention that primitive Christianity was apocalyptic and little else. The solution of what was at first a disappointment and a problem was the discovery of the fact that the Spirit was indeed the Spirit of Christ, proceeding, in the language of a later generation, from the Father and the Son.

Another cross-section. Paul is writing to the Corinthians, a versatile, quick-witted, rather feather-brained community, who had just emerged from the profligate way of life which was mostly taken for granted in a Greek maritime city, a way which the tincture of mystery-religion which some of them had picked up had done little to redeem. Some were now genuinely converted, but the old Adam still stirred in them from time to time, and they were also apt to think that spectacular manifestations of what we should perhaps call psychic rather than spiritual gifts had great importance. To them St Paul is found saying:

> No man can say that Jesus is the Lord, but by the Holy Ghost. Now there are diversities of gifts, but the same Spirit.
> (1 Corinthians xii, 3–4.)

He seems to mean that only in the atmosphere of the Holy Spirit is it possible to take such tremendous words upon your lips. The words themselves are a primitive creed – 'Jesus is Lord.'

In another passage (Romans x, 8) he adds to this another article of faith. By this is not meant, of course, that in the meantime he had come himself to believe or had become accustomed to teach an additional, new doctrine. It is merely that in this context he mentions two articles of faith instead of only one. He says:

> If thou shalt confess with thy mouth the Lord Jesus, and shalt believe in thine heart that God hath raised him from the dead, thou shalt be saved.   (Romans x, 9, 10.)

This was the essential core of early Christian teaching, the Lordship of Jesus, the Risen Jesus. To this faith Saul had himself been brought on the Damascus road, the faith that Jesus had conquered death, and was the Master who claimed his life-allegiance. From this germ came in course of time the Nicene Creed.

It came by way of the further analysis which can be found in other parts of the New Testament. The subject-matter of this further analysis need not be in the present context examined in detail. It must be enough to say here that the Creed is a digest of New Testament theology. The importance of the bits of evidence so far adduced is that they demonstrate that a movement, a theology, was going forward. There really were some Christian believers, and this was the gist of what they believed.

Let us begin again with another cross-section or rather a series of such. The Book called the Acts of the Apostles purports to describe the life of the early Church, at first in Jerusalem, under the leadership of Peter, and eventually, in ever-widening circles, as it was carried by Paul through the cities of Asia Minor, Macedonia, Greece, and eventually to Rome. The writer depends to some extent on his own recollections, and a travel-diary which he seems to have kept during the periods when he was with St Paul, and on what he has learned from such records and recollections of others as were available. He is a careful historian, and though in the speeches which he includes he may have followed the accepted practice of ancient historians, including Thucydides, and have written what he supposes that the speakers might have said, they are all extremely appropriate to their circumstances, and he may have possessed in some cases notes taken by himself or by some other eye-witness. His political and geographical information is very accurate. He names correctly, for example, the different kinds of magistrates who existed in the several cities.

He describes the gradual expansion of the Church to Samaria, and thence, by way of Antioch, into the great world beyond. His method is eirenic. He does not believe in reviving in detail the memories of past controversies. His account of the momentous Council of Acts xv is like the judicious minute book of a committee, which is content to say, 'After considerable discussion, it was resolved. ...' It appears from St Paul's Epistle to the Galatians that it was

B 2

an acute crisis, and that the matter, before the date of the Council, had been hotly and even stormily debated, but in Acts we hear of little but the conclusion.

The purpose of the author is to illustrate our Lord's words, 'Ye shall be my witnesses, both in Jerusalem, and in all Judaea, and in Samaria, and unto the uttermost parts of the earth.' To Jerusalem by Peter and his fellow-Apostles, to Samaritans and to the Ethiopian eunuch by Philip, to Cornelius by Peter, to heathen Gentiles at Antioch by some unnamed evangelists, and presently, by St Paul and others, to the world, the name of Christ was made known. The crossing from Asia to Europe in Acts xvi was not at the time so interesting as it seems to us, because the distinction then between Asia and Europe was not important, but the author rightly lays great emphasis on St Paul's arrival at Rome, where he leaves him, a prisoner indeed, but at the heart of the Empire.

The masterly analysis of Professor C. H. Dodd has shown that the early speeches of St Peter in the Acts, which he believes to be based upon material which proceeded from the Aramaic-speaking Church at Jerusalem, reveal the existence of a *Kerygma* or message proclaimed. It consisted of five points and a conclusion:

(i) The age of fulfilment has dawned. 'This is that which was spoken by the prophets.'

(ii) This has come about through the life, and death and resurrection of Jesus.

(iii) By virtue of the resurrection, Jesus has been exalted at the right hand of God, as Messianic head of the new Israel. 'God has made him both Lord and Christ.'

(iv) The Holy Spirit in the Church is the sign of Christ's present power and glory.

(v) The Messianic age will shortly reach its consummation in the return of Christ.

Finally, there is always a practical appeal: 'Repent, and be baptized, and you shall receive forgiveness and the life of the age to come.' That is what the author of Acts meant by 'preaching the Kingdom of God', and this is almost identical with the message that St Paul subsequently proclaimed.

It is to be noted that the word used by Professor Dodd is *kerygma*. The verb is *keryssein*, to proclaim or preach. There is in the New Testament a clear distinction between preaching and teaching. Preaching is proclaiming, the act of a herald, who announces news. The people of the early Church went about crying, 'Stop! Listen! Have you heard the News? This is what God has done!' Teaching is given to persons who wish to know, or at least are willing to be informed about, the theological or ethical significance of the events which have been proclaimed and are either accepted or in course of being accepted as historical and significant. Occasionally there is also what is called apologetic teaching, the commending of Christian belief to persons who are not yet convinced.

This is a very brief sketch of what primitive Christianity, as glimpsed here and there in early documents and in the first published volume of Church History, was like. Now, with this in mind, let us turn back to the Gospels. Does it seem that the story that they tell was likely to lead to the results which we know to have followed? It is certain, for example, that a Church was founded at Corinth at an early date, and that the Corinthians believed and did this and that. Do the Gospel incidents provide what logicians might call a *vera causa* for what happened afterwards at Corinth and elsewhere? If they do, you have good reason to believe in the substantial accuracy of the Gospel-record.

There are four Gospels. Mark represents the earliest attempt to grapple with the intensely difficult task of presenting on paper the stupendous paradox of the Divine Saviour fulfilling His earthly mission in circumstances of obscurity, opposition, and, in the end, tragedy and seeming failure. Matthew has the best and clearest account of the Master's teaching, and of His relation with the traditional religion of His day. John sees it all *sub specie aeternitatis*. In his pages a clearly Divine Person moves and speaks with transcendent authority. His point of view was such that it tempted him at times to forget the humiliating tension which Mark was at pains to underline, but he is, not temperamentally but in conscience, genuinely historically-minded, and his account of the Crucifixion, though his Figure on the Cross is more majestic than that of the Synoptists, is perfectly realistic.

The book with which an unaccustomed reader should begin is the Gospel of St Luke. It was written for an enquirer, or anyhow a neophyte. It was written for Gentiles, and, except for a comparatively small number of Jewish race, all modern European people, ethnically, and many religiously, are Gentiles. St Luke's Gospel is good reading. It is literature, as Mark is not. His delicate psychological touches are only to be discerned by careful readers. It is impossible to say whether they are due to the Evangelist or his Original, but they appear in his pages. Thus, the Parable of the Good Samaritan begins with a lawyer asking 'And who is my neighbour? Show me who has a claim on me, and I will discharge it', and it ends with, 'Which now of these three, thinkest thou, *was neighbour* unto him that fell among robbers?' In the Prodigal Son the elder brother says indignantly '*This thy son*, which hath devoured thy living with harlots', and the father replies, 'It was meet that we should make merry, and be glad; for *this thy brother* was dead, and is alive again; and was lost, and is found.' St Luke is a truly versatile writer. He can pass, after the four verses of his Preface, which are in the flowing classical style, comparable to the periods of Gibbon, to two chapters in the style of *Pilgrim's Progress*, and then resume his own normal Greek. In Acts he describes the primitive scene of the early chapters in Hebraic language, and his style, as St Paul goes through the world and finally ends at the Imperial City, becomes more and more Hellenic. Or, to take one more example, are there in English any words more beautiful than the last two verses of the *Benedictus*:

Through the tender mercy of our God : whereby the day-spring from on high hath visited us ; to give light to them that sit in darkness, and in the shadow of death ; and to guide our feet into the way of peace.

This is a digression, a tribute to the superb craftsmanship of the Evangelist. Yet it is not altogether out of place, because, if it be asked, 'How did it all begin?' St Luke supplies the answer.

He says that it began like this. In the sixth month of the pregnancy of Elizabeth, the wife of an old country priest, living among the Judaean hills, the angel Gabriel was sent from God to a virgin espoused to a man whose name was Joseph, of the house of David, and the virgin's name was Mary. And the angel said, 'Hail, thou that art highly favoured; blessed art thou among women. Thou shalt con-ceive in thy womb, and bring forth a son.' 'How shall this be?' 'The Holy Ghost shall come upon thee, and the power of the Highest shall overshadow thee. Therefore also that holy thing which shall be born of thee shall be called the Son of God.' And Mary said, 'Behold the handmaid of the Lord ; be it unto me according to Thy word.'

So, in simple words that will never lose their charm, a Greek physician tells how it all began. The earth-shaking movement, which transformed the Roman Empire and created Christian civilization, begins with a Mother and a Child – and God.

What does the modern world make of his story? A right-wing critic will say that it contains genuine history. He will point out this Evangelist claims to have 'traced the course of all things accurately from the beginning' (i, 3, R.V.), that he has been proved by the researches of Adolf Harnack, Sir William Ramsay, and others, to be a careful historian, and seems from internal evidence to be depending here on information which reached him from the Mother herself, perhaps through the agency of some other woman. The critic of the extreme left will perhaps go so far as to say that no such person as the Mary of the Gospels ever existed, and that she is only a personification of Judaism, or of the Christian Church, or perhaps even of the Mother-concept. The verdict of the right-wing critic, if he is an orthodox theologian, must be tested severely, by himself and others, on the ground that his orthodox theology may incline him *a priori* to accept the traditional view. The verdict of the left-wing critic must also be tested, and, if he is theologically a sceptic, may be altogether vitiated. For, while it is possible for a critic to reach conclusions on purely critical grounds, a critic who has definitely rejected the doctrine which the story enshrines, is incompetent, even if the story be true, to appreciate the truth of it. The question is decided for him before he begins the enquiry. This reasoning is not an attempt to predetermine the cause before it begins. It is not a case of 'Heads, I win; tails, you lose.' It is simply a reminder of the fact that the believing enquirer may be independent. The sceptical enquirer cannot but be biased.

Is it possible to draw the extremes together? The beauty of the story does not by itself prove that it is no more than a haze of legend, because God also is an artist. But it is a picture, and therefore, to that extent, idealized, a work of the imagination. Angels do not have bodies, and supposing – it is a lamentably pedestrian hypothesis – that a sound-recording instrument could have been placed within earshot, it would not have recorded the words attributed to Gabriel. The essential substance of the story is – It was somehow made plain to Mary (of whom there is no sound critical reason to speak as other than a real person) that she was to be the Mother of the Son of God. And in a short book of this kind, where there is no space for careful and prolonged enquiry into either theological or historical problems, the matter must be left there. The words of the Creed are: 'Conceived by the Holy Ghost'. There are those who stumble at this, but could there be a more satisfying description of the entrance of the Saviour into the life of man?

The birth of the Child occurred at Bethlehem. Some

simple-minded critics have been misled by St John vii, 42 ('Hath not the Scripture said that the Christ cometh of the seed of David, and from Bethlehem?') to suppose that Jesus was really born in Galilee, and that the whole Bethlehem story is therefore a later legend. They have not perceived the irony of the passage. The Evangelist knows that his readers would know that the Jews, just when they were most confident, were in error. The irony is of Sophoclean quality.

Further, in some quarters it has been suggested that it is so eminently appropriate that plain shepherds should be the first hearers of such news, that they must be fictional. It is also possible that, for the same reason, the story may be true. Fiction presses events into a mould. The mould may be good or bad, wise or foolish, sentimental or realistic, verisimilar or unconvincing, but it is fashioned by the author. Truth is like a key turning in its own lock.

From that time, with the exception of one incident, we hear no more of Jesus for some thirty years. Foolish people have sometimes spoken of the 'wasted years'. Why, having so marvellous an instrument ready to hand, did God not use it sooner? 'Ready to hand' begs the question. A maturing period is not wasted. Tradition says that Joseph died, and that the special aptitude of Mary's Son, the Carpenter of Nazareth, was for making yokes. Be that as it may, it is certain that, when the voice of Prophecy, on the lips of a second Elijah, was once more heard in the land after many years of silence, and John called the Jewish people to repentance, Jesus, who was akin to John, was among those who came to be baptized.

It was manifestly a high moment in His life. There were anciently those who supposed that Jesus was originally human and no more, and that His Baptism made Him Son of God, but this is one of the few ancient heresies which have found no modern favour. There are no 'Adoptionists' to-day. It is all or nothing. But it was certainly in the exhilaration of this experience that Jesus set Himself, alone, in the wilderness, to determine His course of future action.

Temptation – not the ordinary vulgar temptations to be selfish, or lazy, or what not, which are enough for most of us – was not wanting. They are all 'Messianic' temptations. He feels within Himself what may be called at least unusual powers. Is He to exercise them to satisfy ordinary human needs? Secondly, is He to attempt to make the traditional Messianic appearance, riding on the clouds of heaven, so as to compel belief? And, lastly, is He to put Himself at the head of a patriotic rebellion against Rome? There was no doubt something to be said for all these expedients, but the answer was – For the Kingdom of God *Non tali auxilio*. The Kingdom must be built on other, surer lines than those. And on those other lines He begins His further work. Sir John Seeley in *Ecce Homo* has some illuminating words on this scene in the wilderness.

Is it essential to include in a book called *Christianity* some account of Christ's advent to the world of men and of His manner of life therein? Yes, it is utterly essential. There were ancient Gnostics who said, and there are modern Gnostics who say, 'Why this entangling alliance with history? Let us keep ourselves in tune with the Christ-Spirit. That will suffice.' It does not suffice. Such a Christ-Spirit is but a projection, and the ropes with which some would bind themselves thereto are ropes of sand. Without the historic Christ there is no Christianity.

What was the impression made by Jesus on His contemporaries? There have been many attempts to gauge this. There are books (they could all be named) which try to compress the abundant and towering personality into a man-made, private mould, which exhibit Jesus as a lecturer in ethics, a charming character who eventually fell a victim to megalomania, a good fellow, helping lame dogs over stiles, a high-minded political scientist, a proletarian revolutionary, a poet, a visionary who expected the end of the world and died broken-hearted because it did not come, and an Influence of whom almost nothing can be known. Moreover, there still survives in some quarters the old

'Gentle Jesus' picture, the long-robed, rather sentimental figure of Victorian church windows.

So far as we are able to reconstruct the impression made at the time, it was one of loving bewilderment. Among outsiders and those who made a casual contact the bewilderment was uppermost. It is perhaps best represented by the remark of the officers sent to bring Jesus before the Sanhedrin for enquiry. 'Never man spake like this man.'

Imagine the case of a peasant-farmer or shopkeeper of Galilee, who had had a talk with a stranger in the streets of Capernaum or Bethsaida. How would he describe it to his wife when he came home in the evening? It might be something like this:

I met a man to-day, called Jesus. We talked. It was the most extraordinary thing. He looked me in the eyes, and I felt that he knew all about me, what I was worth, and what a lot of shabby quality I had about me. And yet, and yet, I somehow felt that he loved me. I can't explain this, but, do you know, as he talked with me, it seemed that He brought God to me, and me to God.

This is, of course, imaginary, but it seems a fair comment on the recorded fact that when a man ran to Jesus and asked how he could win eternal life, 'Jesus, beholding him, loved him'.[1]

Among those who were disciples, the love was paramount, but there was not a little bewilderment. There is an incident in St Mark (iv, 41) which shows this, and also, almost by itself, establishes the general historical accuracy of the Gospel story. In the ship, on the lake, the disciples say, 'Who then is this?' It is the beginning of the Creed. Actually it is not a creed at all. It is only a question. But this is where what is called Christology begins. And it is true. Had there been in St Mark some story of the Apostles sitting round a table and constructing, clause by clause, the Apostles'

1. This interview was, so to speak, a failure, but it was one of the failures that must be, if there is to be any success. Also, it has been suggested that it was a failure only for a time. The young man came back centuries later, and his name then was Francis of Assisi.

Creed, it would be manifest at once that this was a later interpretation. That sort of thing does not belong to this period. That comes afterwards. But there is in St Mark nothing of the kind. There is only a question. Confronted by the overwhelming personality of their Master, the disciples shake their heads and say, 'Well, this passes our comprehension. There is more in this than we can understand. Who can He be?' Is it not exactly what must have happened?

A second stage is reached at Peter's Confession. It may be supposed that the Lord Himself had known all along – with complete certainty from the day of His Baptism by John – that Messiah was at least one of the categories which it was His vocation to fulfil. The category did not exhaust His vocation (any more than it exhausts what Christian people believe about their Master now), because that was to be whatever the Father should determine, but He must fulfil the old expectation before He breaks new ground. So far as others were concerned, this was the first time that anyone had divined the secret. Peter, in an inspired moment, leaps up to the highest category within his reach. Could it really be that the great superhuman figure who for centuries had dominated the imagination of God's people had verily come to life, and was none other than their own Master? Yes, it was true. He could see now the meaning of a hundred things that had impressed and puzzled him. 'Thou art the Christ.'

A third stage is the penultimate act of the drama. The High Priest asked his Prisoner:

Art thou the Christ, the Son of the Blessed? And Jesus said, I am ... but the High Priest rent his clothes, and said ... Ye have heard the blasphemy, what think ye? And they all condemned Him worthy of death.

That was decisive. It was not in itself a judicial sentence of death. The court had no capital jurisdiction. But it prompted the argument addressed later to Pilate:

'If thou let this man go, thou art not Caesar's friend:

whosoever maketh himself a king speaketh against Caesar.' Again, later, Pilate saith, 'Shall I crucify your King?' The chief priests answered 'We have no king but Caesar.' It was the reason for His Crucifixion. If the Prisoner had found it possible to disavow or withdraw all such claims, there is no doubt that some face-saving expedient could have been found, and on the next day they would have not three crosses on the hill of Calvary, but two.

It was not so. 'They crucified Him, and the malefactors, one on the right hand, and the other on the left.' Then came what in this connexion is the fourth stage of the unfolding of the truth, the Resurrection.

There is no space here to present the evidence for believing that the Resurrection of Christ did really occur. The evidence is considerable and the examination of it has produced in some unprejudiced and even rather unwilling critics an intellectual conviction of its validity. But intellectual conviction is not the whole story. Believers must feel that the conclusion does not sin against reason, but the kind of conviction that might conceivably have been forced upon Pilate or the centurion would not be Christian faith.

The strongest single argument for belief is the fact that Christianity began. A handful of despairing people, without much natural initiative, were suddenly quickened into a tumult of enthusiasm, which has communicated itself to successive generations ever since. Believers have been told or have read that Jesus, on the third day, rose in Joseph's Garden, and they have found that He is Risen in their hearts.

To this twofold appreciation the greatest contributory element will always be Peter's conviction, expressed on the Day of Pentecost:

Whom God raised up, having loosed the pangs of death, because it was not possible that he should be holden of it.

The Resurrection, thus accepted, not merely as a credible but as an inevitable thing, carries with it nearly all the so-called miracles recorded in the Gospels. A few of the incidents can very easily be 'rationalized', and may be misunderstandings of what really occurred, but inasmuch as it is certain that the Corinthians a little later possessed 'spiritual gifts', it is only necessary to reflect on the distance between the Corinthians and St Paul, and between St Paul and Christ, to make it natural to suppose that, when the Lord of life was present upon earth, disease and even death fled at His approach.

There is a highly significant word in Romans i, 4:

Who was declared to be the Son of God with power according to the Spirit of Holiness, by the resurrection of the dead.

The significant word is 'declared', *horisthentos*, 'designated', 'marked out as'. The situation indicated by the word is this – after the Resurrection the disciples said, 'Ah, yes, now we begin to see the meaning of all the things that the Master said and did while He was with us in the flesh. They might have said with Browning's St John:

What first were guessed as points, I now knew stars.

This is perhaps the real meaning of the famous exclamation by Thomas, after the facts of the Resurrection had been made sure, 'My Lord and my God!' It seems to many an improbable thing that one of the Twelve should actually use such language only a week after the first Easter Day, but the Evangelist perhaps means that this was what the Resurrection did in truth reveal. It is in that case a historical anachronism, but sound theology. The impression made on the disciples by the Resurrection of Christ was such that there follows from it the Pauline analysis, and eventually the Logos-theology of the Fourth Gospel.

4

The Significance of the Record

THE version of the Gospel-story offered by Ernest Renan in his famous *Vie de Jésus* had a considerable vogue. In his own country it appealed by its sentimentality, in England because it appeared to provide a credible explanation of what the so-called Liberalism of the nineteenth century found it difficult to accept in its traditional form. There was another contemporary reconstruction – or rather, in that case, demolition – of the story, by D. F. Strauss, which dismissed the history as an example of a supposed myth-making faculty and evacuated the theology by assigning the recorded experience of Jesus to a mystical idealized humanity. This never became well known in England, and it was less plausible. The version of Renan, to those who came to it without much of what St Paul calls the shield of faith, was easy to believe. The theory was that a young Rabbi, of exemplary character and engaging address (*ravissant* was one of the words in the author's vocabulary) proclaimed his message so eloquently and so attractively, and gathered such enthusiastic crowds of hearers, that He eventually began to entertain extravagant beliefs about Himself. A popularized English version of the continental criticism of the period with an appearance of high spiritual value, but one that rested on insecure theological foundations, can be found by the curious in Mrs Humphry Ward's *Robert Elsmere*.

The Renan version is not merely untrue. It is almost the opposite of the truth. The earliest Gospel, that according to St Mark, said by a very ancient writer to contain the recollections of St Peter, when carefully examined, proves to have the same underlying convictions as those which underlie St Paul's Epistles. St Mark's Gospel is not a biography of our Lord. If it were, it would not be a very good one. It was written in order to resolve a theological conundrum, a question beginning with 'Why?' St Mark's answer is a statement of the primitive message of Christianity. And the primitive message is this – that the Son of God came from heaven to destroy the works of the devil, and make men the sons of God and heirs of eternal life. To this end He faced the humiliation of life on earth, and, above all, the extreme humiliation of death on the gallows. St Mark's Gospel, which, as Professor A. R. Ropes of Harvard has remarked, is 'as theological as that of John', was written to exhibit the tension existing all this time between the divine nature of the Saviour and the humble, and, indeed, in the end, degrading circumstances of His earthly career. John Mark, writing his Gospel, might actually have had before him the famous Pauline passage:

Let this mind be in you which was also in Christ Jesus, who, being in the form of God, counted it not a prize to be on an equality with God, but emptied himself, taking the form of a servant, being made in the likeness of man; and being found in fashion as a man he humbled himself, becoming obedient even unto death, yea, the death of the Cross. Wherefore God also highly exalted him, and gave unto him the name which is above every name, that at the name of Jesus every knee should bow, of things in heaven, and things on earth, and things under the earth, and that every tongue should confess that Jesus Christ is Lord, to the glory of God the Father.

St Mark's Gospel is as theological as all that.

Did Jesus then say all this to the Twelve? There was a time when the orthodox answer was almost 'Yes'. Liddon in his famous Bampton Lectures lays hold of every scrap of evidence, using the Fourth Gospel in a way which would now be called uncritical, contending, with a splendid passion of faith, that our Lord accepted every token of respect and admiration, like that of the kneeling leper, begging to be healed, as tributes to His divinity. Liddon was frankly always the advocate rather than the judge. A sharpened historical sense has made modern Christian scholars more judicial. They do not topple over, as does at least one living divine, and snatch eagerly at all the negative arguments on the other side, but they try, not coldly or heartlessly, but fairly and judicially, to reconstruct the historical situation.

Thus the answer to the question – Did Jesus say all this to the Twelve? – is, By no means. It is the theological background of the story. The Gospels themselves contain what may be called the raw material of Christology. They illustrate the Johannine saying, 'I have yet many things to say unto you, but ye cannot bear them now.' As Bishop Gore puts it:

> We can conceive nothing further from the method of Jesus than that He should have startled and shocked their consciences by proclaiming Himself as God. But He had something which in the long run would make any other estimate of Him hardly possible.

Archbishop William Temple put it this way:

> If, standing before them in the flesh, He had said to those devout Jews, 'I am God', He would have reduced them to mere bewilderment.

Even St John, whose Christ moves across the pages of his Gospel with greater and more conscious majesty than the Christ of the Synoptic Gospels, confines his full and rich Incarnation-doctrine to his Prologue. The light of the Prologue shines across the pages of the whole book, but the substance of it does not enter them. The nearest approach to such entry is x, 30: 'I and the Father are one' (the pronoun is neuter – 'one thing' rather than 'one person'), but even here the context ('no man shall pluck them out of my hand ... no man shall pluck them out of the Father's hand') is the voice of One giving spiritual reassurance rather than making a dogmatic pronouncement.

The essential element in the actual picture of the Gospels is a strange combination of utter personal humility with far-reaching, almost boundless claims. No other religious teacher has ever centred His teaching so wholly on His own personality, and at the same time so consistently preserved what may be justly though rather prosaically called an absolutely 'correct' attitude towards God. In saying, 'He that receiveth you receiveth me,' Jesus places Himself behind all the sons of men, their representative. But the words are immediately followed by, 'He that receiveth Me receiveth Him that sent Me,' which is the equivalent of the Johannine, 'I am the way'. A famous passage, which occurs in the oldest and most unshakable stratum of the Synoptic Gospels, and, incidentally, has the Johannine ring about it, contains the same suggestion of being a representative:

All things are delivered to me of my Father: and no man knoweth who the Son is, but the Father; and who the Father is, but the Son, and he to whom the Son will reveal him.

It is followed in St Matthew by another passage which may or may not be from the same ancient source:

Come unto me, all ye that labour and are heavy laden, and I will give you rest.

The words do not in themselves amount to a claim of divine status, but the conclusion is, so to speak, hovering in the margin, waiting to be drawn.

It was drawn later. And if it should seem strange, or incredible, that men should draw conclusions about Jesus which Jesus Himself did not draw in so many words, consider another case. There is no doubt in human history one person who is in fact the best and most noble of all the sons of men. We do not know who it is. It may be Francis of Assisi. It may be some utterly unknown man or woman, living in a back street. Supposing that it is Francis, it may be that posterity will boldly pronounce the verdict, and it may be a true verdict, that he was indeed the best of men. Francis himself would never have done that. Partly because he could not know, and partly because it would be wholly foreign to his character to say anything of the kind. It would rob him of the humility which is his greatest charm. Yet, posterity might say it. The comparison helps to dispel the alleged difficulty of the question 'Why did Jesus, if He was what Christians affirm Him to have been, not say so?'

This is only an illustration. The answer is surely that the Divine Saviour, in the incarnate state, could not possess the actual consciousness of being God, because such consciousness involves having relations with the entire created world and accordingly could not be possessed by a being whose nature was genuinely human without destroying the genuineness of that nature. In fact, the theological analysis of the case is like a sailor's knot; the more you pull it, the tighter it becomes. The more stoutly you believe that the Word was made flesh, the less can you believe that 'the Word made flesh' contravened the conditions and limitations which He had Himself accepted. Von Hugel said, 'Jesus is conceived by the Christian Church as Christ in a sense far transcending that of the Jewish Messiah. Jesus here is declared to hold in His human mind and will as much of God, of God pure, as human nature, at its best and when most completely supernaturalized, can be made by God to hold, whilst remaining genuine human nature still.' To indicate the extent to which the human mind of Jesus was conscious of this, the biblical terms 'the Son' or 'the Son of Man', or such modern terms as 'unique' or 'representative' or 'universal' are as far as we can go. St John's gospel, although it is more of a theological interpretation than a chronicle, and contains some after-thoughts read back into the period, touches a real point with 'I have yet many things to say unto you, but ye cannot bear them now. Howbeit when he, the Spirit of truth, is come, he will guide you into all truth.' Chief of the 'many things' was what is called Christology.

The sort of material with which the early theologians were faced, from which they drew their startling, but, as it seemed to them, inevitable conclusion, included scenes like this: Seventy disciples, sent out two and two into every city and place whither Jesus Himself should come, returned, full of exhilaration, reporting that 'The devils are subject unto us in Thy name'. He said unto them:

'I was beholding Satan fallen as lightning from heaven.'

A mysterious answer. If it refers to the traditional fall of Satan before the creation of the world, it clearly has gigantic implications. If, as seems more likely, it refers, not to a pre-mundane state, but, to the current period, and means, 'While you, on the circumference, were reaping the harvest, I, at the centre, was locked in conflict with the very principle of evil', it claims for Jesus a place at the heart of the world of reality. The disciples were like delegates to a Peace Conference who are pleased because they have secured a five per cent reduction in armaments all round, or a promise that open cities shall not be bombed more than, say, once a week. The voice of One who is much nearer reality than that reminds them that the trouble has an evil root. Is it wonderful that the early interpreters drew large conclusions about a Master whose insight gave Him so wide a range and such deep penetration, who seemed in such vital contact with the moral forces of the universe? We are told by the Logical Positivists and the Existentialists that the ancient and lofty region which is called Metaphysics, where Plato and Aristotle dwelt, has become irrelevant, but there are many who believe that it is still indispensable. This passage is one of those which lead theologians to draw metaphysical conclusions about the place in the scheme of reality first of Christ and then, by inference, of the Father from whom He claimed to come. In fact, there are not a few believers who are aware of the reasons for holding a theistic faith and do not question their cogency, but nevertheless themselves believe in God because they have believed first in Christ.

Then there is that mysterious episode called the Transfiguration, which is dismissed by some as obvious legend, and claimed by others as the classical example of materialization of the spirits of the departed. What are we to make of it? There are some significant details in the narrative which may make us pause before discarding it wholly, or handing it over to those who are more concerned to establish the fact of *post mortem* spirit-activity than to ascertain the truth about Jesus. There is the curious comment of St Mark, 'so as no fuller on earth can so whiten them', which looks like the reminiscence of an eye-witness, the sort of trivial thing which does come sailing into the mind even at solemn moments. There is the rather futile suggestion of Peter, the traditional eye-witness behind St Mark. 'It is a good thing that we are here. Let us make three tabernacles.' It arises from a misunderstanding, but a misunderstanding which belongs to the time of the experience and not to later consideration of its meaning. Finally, there is a whole series of considerations which would not have seemed relevant in the nineteenth century, but in the psychological age in which we live to-day have great importance. They are admirably put by Miss Evelyn Underhill in *The Mystic Way*, p. 114. The nineteenth century had a closed system of 'natural law'. It is out of date, but many are still imprisoned in it. Miss Underhill points out that 'the quiet change of attitude which has taken place among rationalistic scholars during the last twenty years (i.e. 1893–1913) in regard to the stigmatization of the Saints ... is a warning against premature judgement in such matters as "levitation", foreknowledge, or the curious self-radiance said to be observed in ecstatics of a certain kind.' It is, of course, conceivable that the Transfiguration story is merely something which, in the minds of the Evangelists, ought to, and must surely have occurred, but it is also possible that the restraint which characterized the Incarnate life of the Divine Being was for a moment lifted. When our Lord said in the Upper Room of that which He was holding in His hand, 'This is My Body', He was plainly claiming to transcend the ordinary categories of human life. The Transfiguration in like manner may have been designed to prepare the minds of Peter, James, and John to receive the revelation, said to have been uttered by a voice from the cloud, 'This is My Beloved

Son; hear Him', and it is further wholly in keeping with the general *ethos* of the Gospel-story that Moses and Elijah are said to have talked with Him of 'the decease which He was shortly to accomplish in Jerusalem'.

Another supposed problem arising from the alleged silence of the Gospels can be approached in the same way. St Paul, and with him stand in this matter the authors of 1 John, 1 Peter, and the Epistle to the Hebrews, has a doctrine of what is called Soteriology, a doctrine of the efficacy of Christ's Death as a Sacrifice. It is perhaps necessary to premise that neither St Paul nor the other writers say all the things which were said later on this subject. There is much in later Atonement-theology which is neither scriptural nor true, and by some of it scrupulous consciences have rightly been offended. Nowhere, for example, does the New Testament say that sinners were let off their punishment by the substitution of another victim, or that a price was paid to Satan for their deliverance. Nowhere does it say that all mankind, with the exception of an unknown number of predestinate elect sons, are doomed to eternal damnation. The word 'redeem' is indeed constantly used. And 'redeem' means literally 'buy back'. There was further, a Jewish custom by which the first-born, son or animal, was conceived to be due in sacrifice to God, and was 'redeemed' by the substitution of another victim. But the dominant use of the word in the Old Testament is in connexion with two great events in Israelite history, the Exodus from Egypt and the Return from Captivity in Babylon. In neither of those cases was any price paid, and Pharaoh in particular is thought of as robbed and spoiled. Thus the word, in its main and classical use, means 'Rescue, emancipate, deliver'. Mankind was in the clutch of Satan, but Christ saved them from it.

An illuminative Pauline passage is Romans iii, 24–26:

Being justified freely by his grace through the redemption that is in Christ Jesus; whom God sent forth to be a propitiation, through faith, by his blood, to show his righteousness, because of the passing over of sins done aforetime, in the forbearance of God.

The governing words here are 'righteousness' and 'passing over of sins done aforetime'. The Cross, says St Paul, is a manifestation, not only, as is constantly and truly said, of the love of God, but of His righteousness, or justice. This is closely connected with the passing over of old sins. Sins had been committed, mortal and venial, for centuries. The page of human history was black with the evil record of lust and pride and selfishness and cruelty and lies. And God apparently did nothing. It seemed that He did not care. Well, here, says St Paul, is the great sign that God does care. Sin is a thing so vile and so infectious and so poisonous that it brought God the Son to this. Man could not of himself win the victory. Accordingly, the Son of Man, alone, unarmed, except with the perfection of His human nature, fought and won the battle against evil: Christ, not the Agent of any deal or bargain with the evil one, but Christ, the Emancipator, Christ the Deliverer, or, to use words which form the title of a recent famous book, *Christus Victor*. Or, as St Paul puts it in one audacious phrase, when he desires to indicate the mysterious self-identification of the Redeemer with that sinful human nature which was to be redeemed, 'Him who knew no sin, God made to be sin for us, that we might become the righteousness of God in Him' (2 Cor. v, 21).

But was all this not the invention of St Paul or some other theologian? What is the evidence of the Gospels? What does Christ say of it Himself? In the Gospels you have in this matter exactly what you have in the matter of Christology, the raw material of later definition. There is first the general suggestion that the Son of Man stands behind all the sons of men, a suggestion which St Paul later clarified in the pregnant phrase, 'The second Adam'. Charity shown to one of the least of His brethren is shown to Him. Thus *Laborare est orare*. Conversely, an act of spectacular devotion, the pouring out of costly ointment over the Master's feet, is not really a robbing of the poor. *Orare est laborare*. Or, again, the claim that he that receiveth 'you', or 'one such little child' in my name, 'receiveth me'. Secondly, the scene in the Upper Room recalls, and was no doubt intended to recall, the language of Isaiah liii, the Old Testament passage where the doctrine of Vicarious, or, more truly, Representative Sacrifice, takes its clearest shape. Thirdly, you have a mysterious passage in St Luke xii, 50, where our Lord is heard saying:

I have a baptism to be baptized with; and how am I straitened till it be accomplished?

The baptism was manifestly the baptism of death. In this life He was straitened, that is, narrowed, constrained. His life is lived, as human life must be, in one place only, and at one date only. He cannot make contact with all the people even of His own land and generation, still less with those elsewhere or of another century. The coming crisis will baptize Him into a larger, freer, more universal life, where He will take the wings of the morning, and dwell in the uttermost parts of earthly space and time. The best comment on the story is that the Evangelist who recorded the dark saying also wrote the story of the Pentecostal Return of Christ, in His Spirit, no longer bound by the limitations of human existence, but universalized, ready to belong to all centuries and continents of life. The passage is a sort of intensive and compendious statement of a truth which in more general and diffused form pervades the whole Gospel-story, namely that the shadow of the Cross lies over the life of Jesus all the time.

Finally, you have in St Mark x, 45 (= St Matt. xx, 28) the saying which provides the foundation for all the Pauline Atonement theology: 'The Son of man came not to be ministered unto, but to minister; and to give his life a ransom for many.' Isaiah's doctrine of the Suffering Servant had touched the high water-mark of pre-Christian revelation, but, in the manner of the Gospels, it might be said 'A greater than the Servant is here.'

Having this mine of virgin ore at their disposal, Apostles,

illuminated, as has been said, by the master-fact of the Resurrection, owing no doubt much to the spiritual and intellectual leadership of St Paul, worked at it and produced, not a system of dogmatic theology – there is no such thing in the New Testament – but a further stage in the clarifying of the material and discerning of its implications. We know more of St Paul's share in this than of the others, because he wrote more, but in any case he seems to have been a pioneer and leader. There is, however, no truth in the suggestion that he was the creator of Christianity. The original faith as proclaimed by Jesus, was very far from being a simple 'Believe in God and do your duty' religion.

What then did St Paul do? He began, as we have seen, with belief in the Resurrection and the Messiahship of Jesus. The title Messiah, *Christos*, the Anointed, proved not large enough a term to express his conviction. It broke in his hands, and became, not a title, but a proper name, as it is for us to-day. How then did he proceed? You can see him doing it. He cast about for terms in which to express his faith in Christ. He finds in one place (Colossians i, 15) a surprisingly modern expression, 'Christ, the image (or picture) of the invisible God'. At another time, desiring a strong motive for impressing on the Philippians the duties of humanity and unity, he breaks into the tremendous passage quoted on p. 48. To the Colossians, bitten by the Gnostic itch to people the world between heaven and earth with a whole series of celestial beings, from the great God who is so spiritual that He may not be thought of as the Creator of material things, to a Being, far down the scale, who was material enough to handle matter, he says simply that Christ is the sole essential link and that in Him 'dwells all the fulness of the Godhead bodily' (ii, 9). Christ is 'the End of the Law to everyone that believeth'. Through Him God made the world. He is above all. All things are summed up in Him, things in Heaven, things in earth, and things under the earth: He is the first-fruits of resurrection. He is the everlasting Yea to all the old promises of God in Scripture. By Him the veil which lay upon the heart of one reading the old Scriptures has been taken away. If any man be in Christ, he is a new creature. God through Him reconciled the world unto Himself. He is the Head of the Church, which is His Body, and, as more and more converts are brought in, the Church is more and more built up and Christ is more and more fulfilled. Christ is both the foundation and the top corner-stone of the edifice.

All this is very tremendous. But there is more to come. The culmination of the whole process is the Fourth Gospel.

About the Fourth Gospel, which has been called 'the greatest book in the world', this much at least must be said. It is one of the regrets that attend the writing of this little book that there is no space to do justice to this Gospel. If the impudence of a summary may be forgiven, the view to be taken of it is as follows : The writer, John or some other, was an eye-witness, but he had lived so long in the region of spiritual communion with the Master that he often hardly knew in which world he was moving, the world of historical memory or the world of mystical experience. The distinction between history and symbol has become obscure. There is, however, profound significance in the fact that, being a theologian and desiring to teach theology, he chooses the narrative-form. It was essential in his eyes to make plain that the Gospel was historical.

Every spirit which confesseth that Jesus Christ is come in the flesh is of God; and every spirit which confesseth not Jesus is not of God. (1 John iv. 2, 3.)

He even corrects the Synoptists in a point or two, and his local colouring is accurate. Nevertheless, his narrative is a commentary, an interpretation, and it is sometimes hard to say where fact ends and where interpretation begins. At the same time, it is an inspired interpretation, the true interpretation, which sets on the Synoptic Gospels the crown for which they had been waiting. Accordingly, the course pursued in these pages is not to use the events and sayings recorded in St John *simpliciter*, as historical evidence, on a first survey of the material, but only if they seem to be a just commentary on the more easily verifiable Synoptic story. As commentary, the Fourth Gospel is absolutely indispensable.

What it contributes is, first and foremost, the doctrine or theory of the Logos. The Evangelist is aware that *Logos* is a common term on the lips of philosophers. It meant the life-force of the universe, the strength and stay upholding all creation. It has been remarked that it was about as well-known an expression as, say, Natural Law or Evolution is to-day. Most thoughtful people would be able to give some sort of definition of it, and even the rank and file would know roughly what it meant.

The term had a Jewish history too. In later Judaism the Transcendence, and consequently the remoteness, of God was much emphasized, and it became desirable to find some kind of bridge. The Gnostics filled the space, as we have seen, with their speculations. The later Jews had their angelology, but the angels were only messengers, not mediators. For Jews there was the hope of Messiah, and in the meantime it became common to speak of the Spirit of God or the Wisdom or the Word (*Memra*) of God. Philo had used Logos-terminology in his attempt to bring together Jew and Greek.

St John, familiar with both the Jewish and the Greek literature, had the stupendous idea of using the famous term *Logos* to explain the Incarnation. In this he was helped by a fact of which the Greeks had not made use, which for linguistic reasons was out of reach of the Jews, the fact that Logos is a much richer term than the English 'Word' or Latin *Verbum*. It means both Reason and Speech. Thus in St John it means (*a*) the Inner mind or Thought of God, God as He is in Himself, and (*b*) God as He issues forth from Himself in creation, in inspiration and, finally, in the supreme self-disclosure which we call the Incarnation. All this is behind the first thirteen verses of the first chapter of

St John. Then, in the next verse, comes the great announcement of the News. That Logos, who brought the universe
into being, who was the secret source of all the wisdom that
has been among men, that Logos was made flesh, and dwelt
among us. We knew Him, we heard and saw Him, our hands
touched Him, and His Name in His Incarnate state was Jesus.
To the mediaeval Schoolmen the sciences were a pyramid,
and theology, *regina scientiarum*, was the apex. In the New
Testament St John's Gospel holds that place.

So much for the theological significance of the record.
What of its ethical implication? It is not difficult to see that
the theology involved a revolutionary change in the way of
understanding life. The Jew had been devoted to God and
to the Law. His weakness was a tendency to pride, which
needed to be broken by the discovery that the Cross had
turned Law into Grace. The Greek had been devoted to
beauty, and his principle of life had been self-expression.
His weakness was sensuality, which needed to be, not
annihilated, but sublimated by the discovery that the body
of a baptized Christian was the temple of the Holy Spirit of
Christ.

The revolution involved seeing man in a new light, as one
not only made in the image of God, but as a being whose
nature Christ had taken, for whom Christ had died. Yet
never for his own sake, but always, as they put it, 'in Christ'.
This did not mean that the 'neighbour' to be loved must be
a Christian disciple. He might be anyone. Christ Himself
had been 'the friend of publicans and sinners'. It meant that
they had come to have a wholly new respect for human
personality. They believed in Freedom as no one else ever
had before or ever has since. Freedom to-day is much talked
of, but it has few real friends. Its real friends are the Christians, because they have no mould into which they want to
pour everyone. If it is said of them that they are after all
just like anybody else, because they have their definition of
what man should be, and they want to make everybody like
that, their answer is that Christ is not one type among

many, which it is desired to reproduce. He sets men free, they say, to grow, as far as they have it in them to grow, towards the universal perfection that is Christ. There is room there for kings and communists, wise and foolish, old and young. Christ will not force a conscience, but He will set a sinner free to be his real self. There is in Christianity no high-falutin' talk about man being the measure of all things, only a humble recognition of the fact that Christ is the redeemer of human nature, and that, being redeemable, the personality of every man is to be respected. A principle so revolutionary makes most political nostrums look rather cheap, and in fact rather unnecessary.

That this revolution was actually effected in the lives of at first scores, then hundreds, and then thousands of people is incontestable. The classical Jew-convert is, of course, Saul of Tarsus, the Pharisee, the persecutor, and there is no doubt that for him A and Z had changed places. Speaking of the things of which his fellow-countrymen were accustomed to glory (Phil. iii, 5), he says that he himself had as much of them as anyone. He had been legitimate, orthodox, and zealous. Yet for him glorying had become unthinkable. 'Where then is glorying? It is excluded.' A wholly different kind of glorying, a selfless glorying, had ousted it. 'God forbid that I should glory, save in the Cross of our Lord Jesus, whereby the world is crucified unto me, and I unto the world' (Gal. vi, 14).

The classical Gentile convert is harder to pick. In some respects it is St Luke. We do not know enough of the early life of the beloved Physician to say that he had shared the ordinary Greek view of sex-morals. We only know that he was an artist who had found a new ideal of what was beautiful. In a sense deeper than that of our great English Hellenist, he saw that Beauty was Truth, Truth Beauty, and he found that this was all he needed to know.

For the other, more commonplace side of Gentile conversion it is enough to turn to St Paul's incidental mention to the Corinthians of that from which they had been redeemed.

After a rather grisly catalogue of perpetrators of sins of the flesh and of the spirit (1 Cor. vi, 9, 10) he adds, simply, and, it may be supposed, without fear of contradiction:

And such were some of you. But ye were washed, but ye were sanctified, but ye were justified in the name of our Lord Jesus Christ and in the Spirit of our God.

The new standard had been a surprise to some of them. Many before conversion had been *habitués* of the mystery-religions. These for the most part provided a harmless outlet for religious emotion, but did not interfere with morals. Thersites, the burglar, and Lalage, the prostitute, could attend the mysteries, and have there an agreeable sense of religion, and could then return, refreshed and encouraged, to carry on their trades. The Corinthian converts found, to the surprise of some of them, that for baptized Christians, who were communicants, there was a different, much stricter way of life. The Christian mysteries had implications which were not to be gainsaid. The old Adam stirred in them occasionally, but in the main they rose to it magnificently.

What was the secret? It is indicated by a passing remark of St Paul elsewhere (Eph. iv, 21). He has mentioned various forms of profligacy and he continues, 'But ye have not so learned Christ, if so be that ye have heard him, and have been taught in him, as the truth is in Jesus.' St Paul nowhere else uses the simple human name by itself, but in his use of it here he puts his finger in a new way on a vital spot. It was the Incarnation, the earth-shaking fact that the Supreme Being had assumed human flesh and had borne a human name, that made all the difference.

How did Jesus Himself show that He desired to bring about this revolution in outlook and purpose, or even was aware that He was doing or would do so? Scrupulous to respect all that was good in the old Law, which indeed He came to fulfil rather than to destroy, He nevertheless said that the righteousness of His disciples must exceed that of the Scribes and Pharisees. It was a startling injunction, because they were commonly believed to be the most righteous of men, and if righteousness be defined as the keeping of the Law, they were. Behind it lay the major premiss of His life. And what was that? It is often said that the novelty of the Sermon on the Mount consisted of its penetration into the inner region of motive. 'It was said ... but I say unto you.' That it did so is true enough, but it is not the whole truth, or even the most important part of it. The theme of the Sermon on the Mount is 'God'. Living Himself in daily, hourly, and momentary communion with the Father, it might be said that He began every interview and every task 'In the Name of God', He pursued it in conscious, happy, and unfaltering obedience to God, and He ended it with 'Go with God'. This, He felt, must be the atmosphere of the life of man, and it was the main work of His Incarnate life to bring God to men. He did many things of a more classifiable kind. He founded modern democracy, He taught the world charity, He created a new standard of forgiveness, He healed the sick, and much besides. But these were only by-products. For Himself, and in His passionate desire for men, the beginning, middle, and end of life was God. Honesty, truthfulness, unselfishness, humility, chastity, all these things were good, and they would grow on the tree if the tree were sound, but 'Seek ye first the Kingdom of God'. Your first object must be the perpetual coronation of God as the King of life.

A never-failing sense of the divine presence was the fundamental thing in our Lord's life. He possessed it, and He knew that He was bringing the possibility of it to mankind in a way that had not been seen or known or even imagined heretofore. His 'Fear not, little flock, for it is your Father's good pleasure to give you the Kingdom' (St Luke xii, 32) means, 'Keep what I am giving you in circulation, and in your lives and in the lives of those whom you can reach, God will be King.'

For this reason, while there is abundance of ethical teach-

ing in the Gospels, there is no code. Our Lord does not deal
in codes. He flings out great principles like 'Love your
enemies', 'Forgive until seventy times seven', 'Be not
anxious for the morrow', 'Whatsoever ye would that men
should do unto you, even so do unto them', 'He that is
angry with his brother shall be in danger of the judgement',
and leaves them to fructify in the soil of the conscience.
Codifying was bound to come in the end, and here and there
an editor could not refrain from supplying a touch of it in
the narrative. In St Matt. xviii, 15–17, there is probably an
example of this. The mention of the three 'cases' is probably
not authentic. It was added by the second generation at a
time when it had become constantly necessary in Church
life to apply the Gospel principles to actual cases. In the
Gospels there is no calculation. 'Freely ye have received,
freely give.' In one instance our Lord definitely repudiated
the suggested duty of deciding how much of a common
patrimony each of two brothers should inherit. And the
same would apply to wages or dividends. All that the peti-
tioner gets is a principle, addressed to all within hearing,
'Take heed, and keep yourselves from covetousness' (St
Luke xii, 13–15).

In the authentic sayings there is no arithmetic. There are
strange, unqualified metaphors, which bewilder the prosaic
Western mind, sayings about removing mountains, and
camels going through needles' eyes, and offering the other
cheek to the smiter. We hear these, and are left gaping at
them as we gape at the Beatitudes, but with a little more
imagination it would be as easy to apply them to our own
circumstances, as it is to translate the oil and wine and the
two pence of the Good Samaritan into terms of contemporary duty.

It is the same with the doctrine of the Church. To the
question, Did Christ found the Church? the old answer was
'Yes, of course'. The second answer, given at a time when
institutionalism was distrusted, and it was thought desirable
to resolve Christianity into a sometimes rather arid system

of ethics tinged with religion, was 'No'. The answer to-day is: 'No, because it was founded already.' The People of God had existed since Abraham. Christ recreated it, the New Israel. In the old days, when times were bad, the true succession had often been carried on by a faithful Remnant. Our Lord Himself was the Remnant, the link between Abraham and Pentecost. Historical continuity, thus maintained, was still to be carried on. The New Israel was to do all, and more than all, than the Old Israel had ever done. They were to be the Church, and where even two or three should be gathered together in His name, He would be in the midst of them. Their initial equipment was simple, in the sense that it can very easily be described. There are the principles of continuity and fellowship, and there is Baptism and 'Do this in remembrance of me.' But, there is no word of bishops, priests, and deacons. The Apostles are to be the leaders in the new community, and the Spirit will guide them into all the truth, and will consolidate the community, and make it the Church.

If it is possible to imagine some bold archangel venturing to question this apparent absence of planning, the Lord's reply would surely have been 'They will be guided by my Spirit.' As indeed they were.

In the Epistles the same unwillingness to codify appears. In St Paul it might well have been expected, because he was by training a Pharisee and by nature an organizer. It is true that he had come to have a profound distrust of legalism, and he was sure that the whole apparatus for acquiring merit by observing the Law of Moses, or any law, had been turned upside down, that he had a passionate belief in grace, the only power in the world which does not impair freedom. Yet St Paul might have been a codifier, but for one thing. He had been converted after the Ascension and Pentecost. His Christ was the heavenly Christ. He knew, of course, about the years in Galilee, and alluded to them from time to time. Above all, he thought constantly of the Cross and the Resurrection. Yet his first thought was always of Christ, once crucified, now at the right hand of God, and of the Spirit of Christ in the beloved community. If he had had the experience of Peter and John, it is natural to suppose that the ethical injunctions with which he always ends his epistles would have been something like a commentary on the Dominical Words. In point of fact, they are very far from that. In one place, speaking to the Ephesian elders at Miletus (Acts xx, 35) he clinches an appeal by reminding them of 'the words' (not elsewhere recorded) of the Lord Jesus, how that He himself said, 'It is more blessed to give than to receive', but for the most part in his ethical injunctions he is content to bring to bear the Spirit of Christ upon the lives of those whom he was addressing. A good example is Romans xii. It comes after eight closely-reasoned chapters on the nature and power of faith, and three particularly difficult chapters about the apparent non-fulfilment of Old Testament promises, and the link is 'Therefore'. 'I beseech you therefore, brethren, by the mercies of God, that ye present your bodies a living sacrifice.' Then follows a chapter so rich in counsel that there are clergymen who, being called upon to choose a Lesson to be read on some special occasion, have formed the habit of saying to themselves, 'When in doubt, read Romans xii.'

Where does it all come from? There is no doubt that it is what might be called Christ-centred. In verse 5 the basis of his plea for unselfish co-operation is the fact that 'we are one body in Christ', and the climax of his great appeal in the next chapter, the appeal which precipitated the conversion of St Augustine, is, 'Put ye on the Lord Jesus Christ, and make no provision for the flesh, to fulfil the lusts thereof.' In the fourteenth chapter we have, 'Whether we live or die, we are the Lord's.' Consideration for the consciences of the over-scrupulous is expressed by saying, 'Destroy not by thy meat the brother for whom Christ died.' There is no doubt about the Christ-centredness of the ethical teaching, but it is not commentary on the Gospel-narrative. It all comes flowing out of the spiritual region in which the writer habitually lived. Almost it might be said of him, as it was said of his Master, 'He speaketh with authority, and not as the scribes.' What was meant then was that the scribes were accustomed to refer to chapter and verse of the Law and the Tradition. Jesus knew. When He spoke of the Father, His words were 'as a well of water, springing up unto eternal life'. The source of the well was His own union with the Father. St Paul drew on that which was available to him, and indeed was within himself. He calls it in one place (Eph. iii, 8) 'the unsearchable riches of Christ'.

Another writer, less able intellectually, but made wise by the discipline of life, and with an experience which had been denied to St Paul, more fatherly and without the occasional schoolmaster touch which is perceptible in his more conspicuously gifted colleagues, gives practical counsel. The First Epistle of St Peter is in some respects the most attractive of all the New Testament Epistles. Readers of St Paul cannot but admire him. Readers of 1 Peter are constrained to like him. This is how he speaks:

The elders therefore among you I exhort, who am a fellow-elder, and a witness of the sufferings of Christ, who am also a partaker of the glory that shall be revealed:

Tend the flock of God which is among you, exercising the oversight, not of constraint, but willingly, according unto God; nor yet for filthy lucre, but of a ready mind;

Neither as lording it over the charge allotted to you, but making yourselves ensamples to the flock.

And when the chief Shepherd shall be manifested, ye shall receive the crown of glory that fadeth not away.

Likewise, ye younger, be subject unto the elder. Yea, all of you gird yourselves with humility, to serve one another; for God resisteth the proud, but giveth grace to the humble.

Humble yourselves therefore under the mighty hand of God, that he may exalt you in due time;

Casting all your anxiety upon him, because he careth for you.

Be sober, be watchful: your adversary the devil, as a roaring lion, walketh about, seeking whom he may devour:

Whom withstand stedfast in your faith, knowing that the same

c 2

sufferings are accomplished in your brethren who are in the world.

And the God of all grace, who called you unto his eternal glory in Christ, after that ye have suffered a little while, shall himself perfect, stablish, strengthen you.

To him be the dominion for ever and ever.   Amen.

Here is the note of personal recollection. It is not over-done, as it is in the so-called Second Epistle of Peter, the work of one who wrote what he supposed that Peter might have written. In 2 Peter i, 16–18 the author protests over-much that he was present at the Transfiguration. In the passage of 1 Peter here quoted we have the bare claim to have been a witness of Christ's sufferings. We have in 'Tend the flock of God' a possible echo of the commission given to the Apostle in the scene by the lakeside described in St John xxi. In 'gird yourselves with humility' we perhaps even have a recollection of an earlier scene in the Upper Room, when the Master took a towel and girded Himself, and began to wash the disciples' feet. These things may be coincidence, but they are just what might well up in the memory of an old man of pastoral spirit who wanted to use his own experience to help others.

This chapter is very far indeed from being a complete conspectus of New Testament theology or New Testament ethics, but it is enough to show that the Christians were already what the world presently called them, a *tertium genus*, a third race, neither Jew nor pagan. They had their own point of view and their own way of life, and both were unlike anything else that had ever been known. From Homer to Tiberius Caesar there had been statesmen, poets, artists, students, soldiers, bourgeoisie, and peasants, and there were those strange people, the Jews, who were how-ever an ancient race, with a traditional religion, which could at least be respected. But this was new, and very queer.

5

The Early Centuries

THE early Christians, when they launched out into the deep and faced the Graeco-Roman world as a distinct community, were not popular. They could not expect to be. They were so different. The life of the ancient world was still steeped in the dregs of the old pagan religions, which, though they had lost all spiritual power, still had their social vogue. The Christians were unable to share the life. They could not, for example, frequent the theatre, because the classical theatre had been a temple of Dionysus and the contemporary theatre was not decent. They could not even be good citizens, because the Emperor was acknowledged by orthodox citizens to be a God. In the deepest sense their citizenship was unimpeachable. New Testament writers insist on the duty of civil obedience. The Epistle of Clement of Rome at the end of the first century, written amid cruel persecution, which he describes in realistic terms, has a noble passage about the respect due to secular authority. A second century apologist writes of the Christians that 'they obey the laws, and surpass the laws in their lives.' Yet it was impossible for them to hold office, or even to qualify for recognition as good citizens by casting the conventional grain of incense on the Imperial altar. Thus the State lost their services and they lost the experience of serving the State. They were condemned as misanthropes. It was not that they were censorious, or resented the happiness of others, or even objected to pleasure-seeking in itself, but they felt constrained to keep themselves clean from either idolatry or vice. The result was that they were as unpopular as people would be to-day who disapproved of alcohol, tobacco, football, all kinds of racing, pictures, and all forms of the Christian religion. Their principles, combined with their poverty, made them personally ascetic, and the nature of ancient life compelled them to be Puritan in their reaction to it.

In the main their isolation strengthened their purpose, but in one respect it was a handicap. They could not develop the civic virtues, because they were disfranchised by persecution, and despised as being dirty atheists, who indulged in abominable practices at their secret assemblies. Their own homes were decent and well-ordered, but they were not invited by the authorities to organize Ideal Home Exhibitions.

Actual persecution was at first spasmodic and sporadic. There are allusions to it in the First Epistle of St Peter, in the Epistle to the Hebrews and the Revelation of St John. In the second century it became more serious, and in the third century it was at times, though not by any means continuously, a policy of extermination. The Christians were fond of repeating Tertullian's remark that only the bad Emperors persecuted, but it was not so. The high-minded Marcus Aurelius, gravely offended by what he thought the unpatriotic and stupid obstinacy of the Christians, ordered a severe persecution in Southern Gaul. The Christians were undesirables, and it was a duty to suppress them. By the third century they had become a large community and accordingly, it was supposed, a formidable danger to the Empire. The persecutions of Decius and Diocletian were serious attempts to wipe out the Faith altogether.

The attempts failed, as persecution always fails in the long run. They were even in one great respect a gain. They had the effect of stiffening the morale of the Christians. It is indeed not difficult to see that it needed, and bred, fortitude to go to Holy Communion every Sunday, when the congregation, on leaving the house where the service had been held, might find policemen on the doorstep arresting them on the ground that they had taken part in the illicit and indecent rite of drinking human blood. This was, of course, stimulating. At the same time it had something of a bad effect. It made the Christians of necessity less public-spirited than they ought to have been, and it may have made some of them more pig-headed than God had intended them to be. Iron does sometimes enter into the soul of the persecuted man.

Persecution came to an end early in the fourth century. The Emperor Constantine became a Christian. His motives for so doing were not of the most exalted, but, so far as they went, they were sincere. He was a kind-hearted man, who disliked persecution. It seemed to him that the Christians were too strong to be resisted and that the Empire must come to terms with them. He made some examination of the case for Christianity and concluded that it was the true religion. Accordingly he announced himself a Christian, and promoted the spread of Christianity throughout the Empire.

It has been suggested occasionally that the Christian religion thus owes all its success to the adhesion of an emperor, and that this is a rather ignoble rock for the foundation of a Church. It is in point of fact not the rock on which the Church is founded. The Church had been securely founded long before that, and, in any case, it is certain that if Constantine had not been converted, some other emperor would have come to the same conclusion before long, and the results would have been much the same. The thing was bound to come at about that time.

The really interesting conjecture is about what would have happened if, not Constantine, but Marcus Aurelius, nearly two centuries before, had thought it worth while to make enquiries into the actual belief and practice of the Christians and had been unprejudiced enough to follow where that led him. In point of fact, so far from the con-version of Constantine being an advantage to the Church, it was something of a disaster. The Emperor having been converted, it became rather the done thing to be a Christian. Multitudes of half-baked converts poured into the Church, and brought some of their paganism with them. The moral

71

standard of the Christians, which had been kept at a high level during the era of persecution, dropped seriously.

Outwardly, of course, progress was now possible. There had been, so to speak, a change of trumps, and the Christians came out into the public eye. They were now at liberty to build churches. Hitherto they had worshipped surreptitiously in the *atrium* or main hall of some large private house. The new Churches kept to the old architectural tradition of an *atrium*, and were of the basilica type, with a round apse at the east end. Scribes now made large and splendid copies of the Scriptures. Two of those made in the fourth century still survive, *Codex Vaticanus* at Rome and *Codex Sinaiticus*, formerly in Russia, now in the British Museum, which also possesses *Codex Alexandrinus* of the fifth century. These are the earliest complete Greek manuscripts of the New Testament, but the Old Latin Version, made in North Africa, and the Old Syriac Version, from the Middle East, with some recently discovered portions of the Greek text, carry the line back into the second century.

The Canon of the New Testament, that is, the list of books which were received as Holy Scripture, was by now practically complete. Before the end of the first century, Clement of Rome is found quoting St Paul with great respect, but it is probable that he did not think of the Pauline, or any other Christian writings, as the Bible or Scripture, any more than the New Testament writers had themselves. To them 'the Scriptures' meant the Old Testament, and they had no notion that they were writing part of the Bible themselves. By the middle of the second century, the four Gospels, Acts, and thirteen Epistles of St Paul (not Hebrews) were generally accepted as the authorized Christian books. Other books, e.g., Hebrews, 1 Peter, James, etc., were received either in the West or in the East. About the Revelation of St John there was a good deal of hesitation. There were also some other Christian writings, e.g. the Shepherd of Hermas, which were often counted worthy of being coupled with the authorized books. By the time of the

Council of Nicaea the Church was reasonably sure about the books to which it desired to set its seal.

Long before this it had been building up its ecclesiastical organization and its theology. It is not necessary here to enter into the history of the episcopate or of the papacy. It is at any rate certain that at an early period there were 'divers orders of ministers', and that the bishops were thought of as having apostolic authority to shepherd and rule the flock and to lead them in devotion. It was not in theory an absolute authority, as that of St Paul would seem to have been in the Churches which he founded. The bishop was constitutionally encircled by his presbyters, and acted together with them, but he was undoubtedly the centre both of the presbyteral circle and of the larger circle of the Church in his region, and he was treated with great respect. The papal authority developed gradually. The confident medieval exegesis of the famous text in St Matthew, 'Thou art Peter, and on this rock I will build my Church', which took for granted, as not all modern critics do, that the promise was authentic, and further assumed that it was (a) a promise of absolute authority, (b) made to St Peter in person, and (c) intended to endow all future Bishops of Rome, considered as successors to St Peter, with the same authority, was a plant of slow growth, and was not unconnected with the commanding position of the city of Rome in the Empire. The medieval papacy performed a valuable and probably indispensable work but it was not as old as the Church itself.

The theology requires more attention. Organization may be the cement of an institution. Ideas are its life. The sub-apostolic generation exhibits a drop in quality. The writers are good, earnest Christian men and they give excellent counsel, but the supreme note of the New Testament is not struck. Clement of Rome is a disciple of St Paul and Ignatius of Antioch of St John, but almost they remind one of the judgement of Richard Porson, the great Cambridge scholar, when pressed to admire some schoolboy verses.

'I see in them,' he said, 'much Horace and Virgil, but nothing either Horatian or Virgilian.' The bow of Ulysses was too great for them to bend.

In the second century those who are known as Apologists wrote reasoned defences of the Christians against false charges, and reasoned statements of what was taught and believed by them. They used the terms of the Stoic philosophy to explain the Christian Logos-doctrine. The Alexandrians, well read in Greek literature, put forward Christian ideas in a way that they hoped would be congenial to Greek readers, very much as the Evangelist St Luke would have done if he had ever written a theological Epistle to the Gentiles. Origen, whose gigantic learning was carried lightly by an adventurous and powerful mind, boldly took over Neoplatonism and bent it to his purpose.

Then came Nicaea. By that time (A.D. 325) two things had happened. The Christian thinkers were all Platonists (the day of the Christianized Aristotle had not come), and they were familiar with the category of *ousia* or substance. Secondly, the Church had by this time come to include a number of recently baptized pagans, who had not altogether shaken off the old mythology. Accordingly, an idea which no one to-day would believe for a moment gained considerable credence. It was that of Arius, who suggested that Christ was divine, but in some inferior sense. Belief in a Being who is not quite God but very nearly, seems utterly impossible to us, but to the Greeks, nurtured on such stories as that of Apollo, the young god, divine but not equal in power to Zeus, who had become for a season shepherd to Admetus, it was a plausible and easy creed.

Confronted with this suggestion, Athanasius perceived that redemption was at stake. He knew that if Christ truly brought redemption or salvation to mankind it could only be because He possessed it in His own right. Accordingly, he contended inflexibly at the Council of Nicaea for the test word *Homo-ousios*, of the same substance as the Father. The Arians put forward *Homoi-ousios*, of like substance.

Carlyle made fun of the fact that the Christian world was divided over a diphthong, but, when you are measuring, near the vertex, the breadth of an angle of which the arms are going to spread across the world, a millimetre is everything.

Athanasius did not find it easy to persuade the assembled bishops. Many of them were conservatively-minded, and they put forward the perfectly just argument that *Homoousios* was not a scriptural term. Athanasius replied that, when the meaning of scripture needs to be defined, it must be defined in non-scriptural terms, and anyhow the word was essential to safeguard the faith.

He was right, and he prevailed. As the late Earl Balfour said, the adoption of the Arian heresy would have inflicted 'irremediable impoverishment' on the Christian Faith. In fact, it would have destroyed it altogether, because there is no real philosophical defence for such a creed. There is a serious case for believing the doctrine of the Incarnation, but no case at all for believing about seventy per cent of it.

By his victory Athanasius preserved Christianity. The plain man, personified by the French as the charcoal-burner, was, and will always be, unable to understand the profound arguments of Athanasius, but Athanasius saved his religion for him.

The next three or four generations were occupied in Creed-making. Question after question was asked by enquiring and often genuinely puzzled minds, and the Church had to find answers to them. Feeling sometimes ran high, and there were a few discreditable scenes. To put the whole long story in a very few words, the orthodox doctrine of the Incarnation of the Son of God – 'Two Natures, Divine and Human, in one Person' – was conclusively defined at Chalcedon in 461. The Definition of Chalcedon is not familiar to any except scholars and theologians, but it is the official Christian statement. It may fairly be said about this solution that it took the matter as far as it could go, and was the final solution – along those lines. Since then there has emerged a new category, unknown to the old thinkers, that of personality. The use of it has not invalidated the old conclusions but it has dated the method by which they were reached.

For general purposes the Nicene Creed, first drafted at the Council of Nicaea in 325, and subsequently accepted in an amplified form by later Councils, is the sufficient statement of the faith of the Church. The Apostles' Creed, a Western document, which can be traced back in its main substance to the middle of the second century, is a personal creed. It was taught in the West to catechumens who were being prepared for Baptism, and it was repeated by them for the first time as soon as they had been baptized. It is Western, a short, plain, straightforward digest of New Testament teaching, which never became much known or used in the East. The Nicene Creed, which originally began with 'We believe', is the Creed of Christendom. It is Eastern in origin, and it exhibits the Greek power of analysis and close definition, but it soon spread to the West, and has been used ever since as the normal public confession by Christian people of their Christian faith. It is perhaps worth while to add that the decisions of a General Council only become 'oecumenical', that is, of universal authority, as they are gradually accepted by the whole Church in practice. Their authority does not depend on the numbers or representative character of the Council but on acceptance of the Church, which is, of course, a matter of time.

Why must there be creeds? It is sometimes supposed that there was in the fourth and fifth centuries a sort of lust for creed-making for its own sake. In point of fact, the Creeds are all defensive in origin. They were made because questions had been asked, and answers had to be found. The Church had to dig down into the meaning of New Testament language and of its own experience, and find an answer to what Arius, or Apollinarius, or Nestorius, or Eutyches was suggesting. The simple, primitive Apostles' Creed had been content to say:

I believe in Jesus Christ, His only Son, our Lord.

This is enough for everyday purposes, for an individual professing his own Christian faith. But sharp-witted men arose and said, 'But what exactly do you mean by this? Is Christ truly divine, in the full sense? What is His relation to the Father? And to mankind? Was He created? Is He eternal? Was there ever a time when He was not?' These questions were actually asked, and it is clear that something had to be done about it. The answer was the Nicene Creed. The first draft of it had at the end an anathema pronounced on those who believed otherwise, but this happily disappeared in the subsequent revision. It is a positive statement of the Church's faith, and passes no judgement on those who are unable to receive it.

Three more points remain to be made: (1) The word 'substance' is difficult to modern ears, because it suggests solidity. The Greek *ousia* simply means 'essential nature'. The word *essentia* never became a common Latin word. *Substantia* was regularly used, and from this comes the misleading English term. (2) The pith and marrow of the Nicene Christology was put by Professor Gwatkin in simple words: 'Christ, as Divine as the Father, as Human as ourselves.' (3) 'Came down from Heaven' is, strictly speaking, a metaphor. Heaven is not a place, above the earth, from which it is possible literally to descend, but a state. Heaven is where God is or where the pure in heart see God. And 'came' is a local term. The purpose of this clause is to express the notion of *Arrival*, the arrival of that which had not been there before, of that which could not have come from any other quarter, a divine reinforcement of human strength and virtue, not the surging up of a new wave, but an accession from elsewhere.

It may well be that a further question will arise in the mind of the reader. The Creeds may be defensive in their origin and the replies to real questions. But why is it all so difficult? The reader might say, if he happened to know what Dr Edwin Hatch once wrote, that in the Sermon on the Mount you have a world of Syrian peasants, and in the

Council of Nicaea a world of Greek philosophers. Why cannot we have the one and leave the other?

The reply is threefold: (1) Behind the teaching of the Sermon on the Mount – 'It was said . . . but I say unto you' – there lies a profound metaphysical question – What is the status of the Speaker of these bold words in the world of reality? (2) The Nicene Creed contains difficult metaphysical affirmations. But they are no more difficult and no more metaphysical than the affirmations of St Paul and St John. (3) The exposition of so momentous an affirmation as that of the Divinity of Christ cannot but tax the intelligence. Can Einstein's doctrine of the relativity of physical measurements, or the argument of what is called by astronomers the Fitzgerald contraction, be expressed in words of one syllable? There is an interesting passage in one of Jung's books about the personality of the poet, which oddly resembles the language of the Definition of Chalcedon. The Church does not require any particular height of brow as a condition of membership, but there must be somebody somewhere who can answer hard questions in a sensible way.

To leave these high matters and return to the general course of Christian history in the ancient world, the moral drop which came with the conversion of the Emperor and the new popularity of the Church was, in a way, countered by a new development. Dissatisfied with the worldliness which was spreading in the Church, some of the keenest spirits went out into the desert and embraced the ascetic life. This, in its early stages, was solitary. The first monks were eremites. Later St Benedict of Nursia gathered men into a community and compiled the first Rule of Common Religious life. From it have come all the Monastic rules, some, like those of the Carthusians, much more severe than that of Benedict, but all dividing the twenty-four hours of the day between the *opus Dei* or corporate worship, labour, which might be either literary or manual, and sleep. The development served to keep alive some of the more obviously heroic qualities of the Christian life, but it also let in the dangerous doctrine of the two standards. There is, of course, a real difference between living according to what are called the Evangelical Counsels, complete poverty, chastity, and obedience, in a religious community, and living as wife or husband in a home in the world. But in so far as it is assumed that the former is the Higher or Perfect Life, and that the other is not a vocation but a *pis aller*, it may lead to pride on the one hand and a lowering of standards on the other.

The spiritual leaders of those who remained in the world – and that was, of course, the vast majority – were very far from accepting a low standard either for themselves or in their teaching. Men like Ambrose and Jerome and Hilary in the West and the Cappadocian Fathers in the East were developing a new Christian ethic. It was not new in the sense of departing from the scriptural pattern, but it was applied to the new conditions in which the Christians found themselves, not now isolated and persecuted, but called to take part in the affairs and public life of the world. The sociology of the Fathers was often intensely socialistic. The existence of property is a concession to human weakness. Wealth is a danger. Almsgiving is bare justice. And they were not afraid to proclaim their doctrine in high quarters.

The great Emperor Theodosius, a devout Christian and a high-minded but occasionally very passionate man, had commanded, as a punishment for a grave breach of public order, a wholesale massacre of thousands of people of Thessalonica. Ambrose, Bishop of Milan, wrote to him:

I persuade, I entreat, I exhort, I admonish, because it is a grief to me that the perishing of so many of the innocent is no grief to you. I dare not offer the sacrifice if you are to be present. ... You are a man, and as you have sinned as a man so you must so repent. No angel, no archangel can forgive you. God only can forgive you, and He forgives those who repent. ... I love you. I esteem you from my heart; I pray for you. If you believe it, accept what I say. If you believe it not, pardon me for preferring God before you.

The Emperor, having received this letter, nevertheless came to Church at the hour of service. Ambrose met him in the porch, and said:

It seems, Augustus, that you have not repented. ... How can you uplift in prayer the hands which yet drip with innocent blood? Or receive into such hands the Body of the Lord? Depart! Add not sin to sin.

The Emperor humbled himself, and did public penance for eight months.

The work of converting men from paganism went on all the time. The Christians had won their battle, and the victory had now to be consolidated. They had begun without resources, wealth or influence. Politically *personae non gratae*, and with a bad social reputation, they proved themselves the better men. As T. R. Glover put it, they out-thought and they out-lived the pagans. And now they were reaping the reward in largely increased numbers. There were some half-converted converts, and they brought in some paganism with them, but the Church was by no means overwhelmed. Great pains were taken with the instruction of catechumens. It was a long and serious business. The lectures delivered by Cyril, Bishop of Jerusalem, towards the end of the fourth century can still be read, clear and interesting expositions of the Creed and of Christian conduct. Of course it was gradual. The Graeco-Roman world was intelligent, sophisticated, and rather weary. The process of consolidation was much more than what soldiers called mopping up. There were no mass-movements, such as occur among simple peasant people. That came later in Northern Europe. During the earlier centuries the peasants were actually the last to be converted. The urban communities became Christian first. And it was by no means a matter of course. Not all the Emperors after Constantine were benevolent. Some were heretical, one, Julian, went back to a deliberate paganism. But the Christians not only had the better case; they were the better men. Modern people who do not know much about Christians often think of them as mild and gentle: the Vicar, a nice old thing, but not amounting to much, and a few pious old ladies with nothing else to do but go to Church at all hours. It would perhaps surprise them if they knew that Dr Gilbert Murray once said, 'Those who are now timid, tender, and reverent in their orthodox world in the third or fourth century would have sided with the old gods. Those of more daring and puritan temper were the Christians.' The Christian was the *enfant terrible*.

After Nicaea, the next very great name is Augustine. He is one of the minds which have changed the history of the world. Before him St Paul had done it, and after him Luther and Calvin, Galileo, Newton, Darwin, and Karl Marx. Immense influence has also been exercised by Homer, Virgil, Origen, Dante, and Shakespeare, and by the military conquerors, but, with the possible exception of Alexander, they did not by their ideas turn the course of history in a different direction. Augustine did. He was the founder of medieval Europe, and he was also the originator, with his left hand, of another idea which remained rather latent for eleven centuries till 'Augustinianism' reappeared as Calvinism. He lived at a time when the Roman Empire was tottering to its fall. Men were saying that the old Roman virtues had been sapped by Christianity. Augustine replied that they had been sapped by soft living and by political irresponsibility. He might have added quite truly that Rome, by exacting perpetual tribute and not establishing industries, had sucked the provinces dry and that the whole structure was perishing of economic inanition.

Augustine proceeded to develop his theory of the two Kingdoms, the Kingdom of the World and the Kingdom of God. His *De Civitate Dei* became the theological and political manual of the Middle Ages. The Barbarians who came pouring in from the North and East and took over the Western Empire imbibed something of his teaching, and when in 800 Charles the Great was crowned by the Pope, the Holy Roman Empire, with its doctrine of the two swords, the sacred and the secular, was firmly established.

Meantime in the East the course of history was more uniform. Constantine had built Constantinople, or Byzantium, the New Rome, and the two Empires, West and East, gradually fell apart. The new city was the capital of the Eastern Empire, and to a great extent also of the Eastern Church. Byzantine Christianity was always very 'Imperial'. Byzantium ceased to be a Christian city when it fell to the Ottomans in the fifteenth century. The flight of the Greek monks and scholars to the West, with their Greek manuscripts, had not a little to do with the Renaissance in Western Europe. The West had known nothing of Greek culture, and, for good or ill, it took them by storm.

The traditional part of the Eastern Emperors in Church affairs was taken over to a considerable extent by the Tsars of Russia. Apart from this secular dominance of the monarch, the Eastern Church was directed by the Patriarchs of Jerusalem and the other ancient centres.

The East was conservative and vehemently orthodox. It prides itself on having preserved the ancient Faith of the General Councils, without addition or subtraction. In fact, the Eastern complaint to this day about the Roman Catholics is that the Pope is a comparatively modern upstart and that Popes have added to the Faith. The East has always been more theologically-minded than the West. The West in early days learned much of its theology from Eastern teachers, just as the ancient Romans had learned about art and literature from Greece, but they reproduced it in a cruder form, and often with more care for the stability of the ecclesiastical structure than for profound theological research. The East had its heresies, even after Chalcedon, but they concerned recondite issues like the nature of the human will of Christ. Apart from such controversies, and from another controversy which raged for a long time about the propriety of setting up images in Churches, the East went on from century to century unchanged. In the eleventh century the ecclesiastical unity of East and West, which for a long time had been strained, broke altogether, and the East went on alone, but much as before. They had no Reformation, and until quite lately Eastern ecclesiastics were uninformed, and uninterested, about ecclesiastical affairs in the West. In recent years what is called the Oecumenical Movement has drawn the East and part of the West together in a new and seemingly very hopeful way. Orthodox ecclesiastics from Russia and the Balkans have taken part in conferences with Anglicans and Protestants at Lausanne, Jerusalem, and elsewhere. It was a great moment when in 1925, 1,600 years after Nicaea, an Orthodox ecclesiastic stood out in Westminster Abbey and in sonorous tone recited the Nicene Creed in its original language. Since 1945 the Iron Curtain has made it very difficult to maintain these newly-found relations or even to know what the situation is.

In the West the centuries that follow Augustine are often called the Dark Ages. They are dark because their story is but dimly known to most modern people, and they are dark because dark and cruel things were done in them. Yet they witnessed great material events, they saw forests cleared and swamps drained, and large portions of the earth's surface made fit for human habitation for the first time. Spiritually, they saw the conversion of Northern Europe. The conversion of England is a fairly typical example of what happened. Britain, like other parts of the Roman Empire, had been Christianized. It is difficult to say how deep the Christianization had gone, because the English wiped it out. The Britons were either exterminated or driven back into the remote West, and England was heathen again. The arrival at the same time of Gregory's mission from Rome and of Celtic evangelists from the North produced a swift result. Kent and Northumbria were converted, Wessex and East Anglia and Sussex followed. Mercia held out for a time, but could not resist the winning grace of Chad. Before long all England was Christian.

The English Christianity of the seventh and eighth centuries was a fine product. It was over-monasticized. Many kings laid aside their responsibilities and went as pilgrims to Rome, where they became monks. And there were some sordid patches. The Penitentiaries of the period reveal the existence of bestiality in places. Yet it was a fine thing. It bred saints like Cuthbert, Aidan, and Bede, Christian kings like Edwin and Oswald. It nourished the heroic, stormy soul of Wilfrid of York. It sent out Winfrid from Devon to become the Apostle of Germany and Archbishop of Mainz.

France was already Christian. The Faith had been planted there since the second century, or perhaps earlier, and there had been no heathen Saxon invasion. True, there were the Normans, but they were quickly converted, and became orthodox, devout Christians in their virile, rather overbearing way. Some of the early Franks, more German than French, for all their name, were rather crude converts. King Clovis, hearing for the first time the story of the Crucifixion, was full of generous indignation. 'Ah!' he said, 'why was not I there with my Franks?' Russia and Scandinavia came later, but the Faith took firm root. Prussia was last of all, and it has been thought – and that not merely as a debating-point of politicians – that the process of conversion there was less complete.

Thus the Dark Ages were not really quite so dark as is often thought. There were vast areas of untilled forest land, and there were regions of brutality and barbarism. The fall of the old Roman Empire was not accomplished in kid gloves. In England the coming first of the English and then of the Danes wiped out first the whole, and then about half, of what had been a Christian culture. Even the Norman, Christian as he was, and regarding his expedition as a holy war, behaved in the traditional conqueror's way, and devastated the North of England so thoroughly that it did not recover – if recovery that be – till the Industrial Revolution. Yet in the period great things were done. It was as if a gigantic creature, leggy, loose-knit, misshapen, not yet arrived at its full size or strength or dignity or beauty, were nosing its way through the thick brushwood of a sombre forest. Some of its movements are ungainly, and some of its habits are unpleasing. Yet it has purpose, and there is promise of both power and grace when it shall reach maturity. Soon it will attain that condition, and will come out into the sunshine, and then we shall see something for which splendid is not too high a word.

6

The Medieval Splendour

WHEN the sun rose on thirteenth-century Europe, its radiance illuminated a rich and generous culture. In certain respects it may even be said to have been a widespread culture. It is true that the mass of the people were illiterate, occupied poor and uncomfortable dwellings, were roughly dressed and lived on monotonous food. They seldom went beyond the bounds of their own parish. But there was nothing machine-made, and even in the poorest houses the earthenware or wooden vessels were of a comely shape. And there was in every village one building that was beautiful and richly adorned. In their homes they had work and food and sleep and the birth and bringing-up of children. The whole of whatever else they had came to them through the Church. And the Church was everybody's home. Money and fine clothes and good food were for the few, but all that the spiritual and intellectual resources of the period could furnish was put at the disposal of the whole population in the Church. Here they touched the great world of literature, science, and art. They knew this only very dimly. Less dimly, they knew their Church to be the House of God. It was there that they were accustomed to 'see God' in the Mass. They lived close to nature, and thus close to God. Harvest really was harvest, the food supply of that parish for the coming winter. This kept them simple and natural. There were class distinctions, insuperable and unquestioned, but in all that mattered most both prince and peasant felt themselves to be in the same boat, and the boat was the Church.

Here and there a Norman church or a Norman castle still lifted its strong towers into the sky, and there were springing up everywhere, as at Westminster, Sarum, Lincoln, or Exeter, churches of a less majestic but far lovelier type, the type that the Gothic spirit found for itself in England. The builders designed and built, not for the comfort or convenience of congregations, but for God. The parish churches, in East Anglia for example, were made much larger and more splendid than was precisely necessary, because the builders wanted the parish to have a great House of God.

The Universities, Paris and Bologna on the continent, and Oxford in England (the relative positions of Oxford and Cambridge were not then what they are to-day), were attracting thousands of eager and sometimes turbulent students, and were imparting to them, in very uncomfortable conditions, the severely logical, and, as it would seem to us, the rather arid culture of the period.

This consisted of an elementary course (*Trivium*) in Grammar, Rhetoric, and Logic, a more advanced course (*Quadrivium*) in Arithmetic, Astronomy, Music (these being studied only as they were required for Church purposes, calculation of Easter, etc.) and Geometry. The student was then ready to proceed to consider the Scholastic philosophy, a course founded on the *Sentences* of Peter Lombard, with rather mechanical 'proof-texts' from the Bible.

Monastic houses, for men and women, abounded. Some of the long established Orders grew rich and worldly, but there were always fresh foundations to renew the original severe tradition, and some Orders maintained the old frugal life and the old continual prayer throughout the centuries. Quite recently Religious Orders of a new sort had sprung up, Friars, Franciscan and Dominican, wandering, barefoot men, who, at first at all events, brought an evangelical breath of cool, refreshing air into the hot sunshine of medieval Church life. In course of time they became rapacious, and a nuisance, but at first they were preachers of a simple Gospel, which was welcome to the countryside. Not a few of both monks and friars were among the University students, where they had hostels of their own, and some of them became great scholars and theologians. The Church, especially the monasteries, owned much, far too much, of English land, but the monks were, at least in personal relationships, good-natured landlords, the country people found them friendly neighbours, and everybody, even the most worldly, even the wicked, approved of their existence and felt grateful for their prayers. Behind them were the Schoolmen, the brains of the Middle Ages, men of consummate intellectual power. Albertus Magnus, Peter Lombard, Thomas Aquinas, and, among ourselves, Duns Scotus and William of Ockham had the whole of the learning that there was at that time, and a superb power of building all knowledge together into a logical pyramid, with Theology, the Queen of the Sciences, at the apex. They were masters of such mathematics, chemistry, physics, and biology as there was, and they drew it all into the service of theology. Their reasoning was logical, and often very abstract. Like lawyers constructing a complicated will for a very large estate, they thought of every eventuality and answered all the questions. Their arguments for the Being of God were all varieties of the argument from motion or change. Things are observed to be in motion. Always there is a cause for this. Push back the enquiry to the beginning, and you find yourself compelled to postulate a First Cause, which is God. Sometimes the reasoning was very abstract indeed, as when Anselm put forward his famous *Quo maius nihil*:

That than which no greater can be imagined must exist, as otherwise a greater could be imagined, namely that same concept in reality.

Descartes years afterwards gave this an easier form when he argued that Existence is good; non-existence is bad, and therefore that which is perfect must exist.

It may sound barren, over-intellectualized, and there are those to whom the God of the Scholastic divines is too much *deus philosophorum*, not one for faith to adore. Yet they never said that they could prove the whole of Christianity by logic.

The existence of God, yes, but the Nature of God, the Incarnation, the Church, the Eucharist, these were matters of Revelation. And they were all the time devout, worshipping churchmen. St Thomas Aquinas wrote the *Summa Theologiae*, but he also wrote Eucharistic hymns of passionate devotion, and a prayer of Preparation for Communion which millions of plain people, of many different allegiances, have used with great happiness. He died at the age of forty-seven, and in the last year of his life he fell into a trance at the altar, after which he refused any more to put pen to paper. It is thus described by Robert Bridges:

When Reynaldus, with all the importunity of zeal
and intimacy of friendship, would have recall'd him
to his incompleted Summa, and sighing he reply'd
'I will tell thee a secret, my son, constraining thee
lest thou impart it to any man while I live.
My writing is at end. I have seen such things reveal'd
that what I have written and taught seemeth to me of small
    worth.
And hence I hope in my God, that, as of doctrine
there will be speedily also an end of Life.'

By comparison with these intellectual giants, the parochial or secular clergy were commonplace enough. Few of them were well educated, most of them had just enough Latin to read their service books, and just enough divinity and common sense to give some useful guidance to their flock. There were some black sheep among them, but most were decent, godly men.

Behind the Schoolmen, and all the ecclesiastics, bishops, priests, deacons, and the monks and nuns and friars, and the hosts of persons in minor orders, comprising all those whom we now call Civil Servants and, indeed, most of those who could read and write, there was Rome. Rome for the West was the acknowledged centre of it all. Her position seemed unshakable. True, there were scandals, especially towards the end of the period. During the greater part of the fourteenth century the Papacy was held captive at

Avignon, and the Popes were both racially and politically French. This, inasmuch as it was the century of the Hundred Years War, did not make the Papacy beloved in England. Then came the Schism, with two rival claimants to the throne of Peter, and it was not easy to decide which was the true Pope. Later, the Renaissance Popes were worldly and often thoroughly wicked men. Indeed, apart from the characters of individual Popes, the Papacy, once a valuable and probably essential point of unity, had become a vast machine, served by innumerable functionaries, clogged with vested interests. The wheels of the machine moved slowly. English kings found it convenient to maintain an Italian agent at the Vatican, and for several generations paid him by making him Bishop of Worcester. Moreover, the wheels of the machine often needed to be oiled. *Venalia Romae omnia* was a common cry, which was not destitute of truth. In England the Papacy was accepted as a matter of course, but it was not popular. The English kings did not like appeals being carried by ecclesiastics from their own courts to Rome, and no one liked the system by which the Pope increasingly claimed to 'provide' clerics, sometimes foreigners, to hold English benefices. Nor did any Englishman like such demands as those which Master Martin, the Pope's collector, made on his pocket.

Yet the great edifice remained. There were a few sporadic outbursts of what was afterwards to be called Protestantism during the Middle Ages, of which Lollardism in England was among the latest, and, in an indirect way, the most successful, but they were all mingled with political heresies, which were novel and unpopular. These were suppressed with a strong hand. The Church did not hesitate to use force, or rather to charge the State to use it. Themselves the victims of persecution for the first 300 years, the Christians, when power was at last on their side, began, some of them, here and there, to use the hateful weapon of persecution against heretics. 'Compel them to come in' was an unhappy malquotation from the Gospels. In the earlier Middle Ages everyone conformed and there was not much need for force. But the officers of the Church were vigilant, and there was always force in the background, which was used more and more, as heresy sprang up. There was a sort of twisted principle in it. They burned men's bodies in order to save their souls and to prevent the disease from spreading. Perhaps it did save their souls, though not quite as the authorities intended. For, if we may adapt the words of the Baptismal rubric, a baptized heretic, martyred before he commits actual recantation, is undoubtedly saved. Even in the days of the Inquisition the burning was technically not the work of the Church. The Church found the prisoner guilty of heresy, and handed him over to the secular arm, with the smug request that there be no shedding of blood. Many of the persecutors were no doubt decent and kindly people in private life, but it was a hideous policy, from which the world has not, even now, shaken itself free. It has existed ever since in the diluted forms of ridicule and social ostra-cism, and it has in recent years reared its Gorgon head again, with far more than the medieval grimness, with far less excuse, and on a gigantic scale.

Meantime, the great machine stood, *semper eadem*. Dante, who, to borrow words used over-generously of Milton in England, was surely 'the God-gifted organ-voice' of medieval Europe, was an Imperialist, no friend of Popes. Yet the Catholic Church, the Body of Christ, was for him eternal, imperishable, the only conceivable instrument of the divine purpose. Its teaching was the truth of God. Dante accepted the Papacy as the necessary crown of the whole structure on its ecclesiastical side, and he never for a moment supposed that it was possible to do without it.

In fact, the whole thing was taken for granted by everyone. Very few had any accurate knowledge of history, and it was commonly supposed that the Church, Pope and Cardinals and all, had always been the same, much as it was assumed by the author of the Books of Chronicles that the whole ceremonial and music of the Second Temple had been in existence under the Kings. Even among the more learned, this was so. When documents were forged, alleging that the Emperor Constantine had desired that the Bishop of Rome should have perpetual primacy, it may have been done. *bona fide*, to supply evidence which must surely once have existed but had somehow become lost. No one asked awkward questions when Transubstantiation was defined, and the Elevation of the Host became the central feature of the Mass. Some were surprised, but hardly any questioned it. The Church had authority, the Church knew. When the usurper, Henry IV, salved his conscience and conciliated the Church by sanctioning the Act *De Heretico Comburendo*, when dying men were pressed to bequeath money to the Church and were assured that it would expedite their passage through Purgatory, nobody questioned it. The Church was right. The Church knew.

A curious example of this occurred in the life of Wyclif. Bred as a Scholastic theologian, Wyclif presently developed a critical spirit. He attacked the avarice of ecclesiastics and the abuses of the system. John of Gaunt, Duke of Lancaster, the King's uncle, was his patron, and supported his anti-clericalism with right good will. Wyclif then turned to theology and questioned Transubstantiation. This was the Ark of God. The Duke was not going to risk his immortal soul by anything of that kind, and dropped Wyclif like a hot potato.

The Duke was a not untypical example of the medieval nobleman, rich, ambitious, unscrupulous, critical of the clergy, but determined not to incur the charge of heresy, and leaving in his will very large sums for Masses to be said on his behalf. For a much more favourable example we can look across the Channel at a rather earlier period, and see the ideal Christian knight in St Louis, King of France. Of him a contemporary admirer says:

This holy man loved God with all his heart and imitated His works; and this appeared in that as God died for the love which He had to His people, he put his body at venture many times for the love which he had to his people, and he could have done otherwise if he had wished.

Dr W. H. Hutton, who quotes the passage, adds:

He had indeed all the delicacy, the delightful inconsequence, of a child, and with it a courage that never faltered in the more difficult times. His devotion was touched by no shadow of weakness. His life of prayer gave him continual strength and energy. He was a doughty knight and in enterprise no man of his time surpassed him. Threats of torture or of instant death left him unmoved ... His fearlessness and his charity remained the striking marks of his character to the end.

St Louis and Joan the Maid are the two glorious figures of medieval France.

To return to England, a man of completely different type, and one darkly suspected in his lifetime of nefarious practices, was Roger Bacon, the thirteenth-century Franciscan Friar. Like other scholastics, he had a general knowledge of all the subjects that were then studied. His *Opus Majus* was an outline of grammar, logic, mathematics, physics (especially optics), experimental research, and moral philosophy. He was very critical of other workers in those fields, but he was an original thinker and experimenter, with a broad view of learning, and he showed singular foresight in looking to the time when spectacles, gunpowder, mechanically-propelled boats, and flying-machines might be used. His sharp tongue and his addiction to alchemy and astrology caused him to be feared as one in league with the devil, but he was never formally condemned, and the traditional picture of Friar Bacon, the necromancer, is a libel. He was a man wholly given to the pursuit of learning, and, though his accumulated stores included some rubbish, he was nevertheless one of the fathers of modern science.

If we turn to fifteenth-century Norfolk here are two women. One, Juliana of Norwich, was an Anchoress, a solitary dweller in a hut or cell in a churchyard, and subsisting on the food passed in by charitable neighbours through the hatch. She was a mystic of remarkable spiritual quality. One of her sixteen 'Shewings' or revelations of divine love was this: 'It is sooth that sin is the cause of all this pain; but all shall be well, and all shall be well, and all manner of thing shall be well.'

Margery Kempe of Lynn was an eccentric. She was a married woman, who puzzled her husband and the neighbours with her alternate extravagant weeping and extravagant exaltation of spirits. She spent her time in

great sobbings and sighings after the bliss of heaven ... so much that she could not well restrain herself from speaking thereof; for whenever she was in any company she would say oftentimes 'It is full merry in heaven!' And they that knew her behaviour beforetime, and now heard her speaking so much of the bliss of heaven, said to her 'Why speak ye so of the mirth that is in heaven? Ye know it not, and ye have not been there any more than we.' And they were wroth with her; for she would not hear nor speak of worldly things, as they did, and as she did aforetime.

A much more normal life than any of the aforementioned was that lived by the Paston family, and described over several generations in the *Paston Letters*. They were a well-to-do family farming their land, interested in the education and prospects of their sons and in procuring good marriages for their daughters, alert to hear news about the king and public affairs, promoting a Christmas mumming of St George, just and not unkindly landlords. It never occurred to them to be anything but Churchmen or to question the desirability of pilgrimages for those who cared about such things, but it also never occurred to them to be extravagant or eccentric in their religion. They were a sober family of God-fearing, prosperous people in what was then the wealthiest part of England. Their underlings never for a moment doubted that the Pastons had been called of God to be masters, and they no doubt served their masters faithfully, with some private grumblings. Only once in all English history did the peasants really rise in revolt, and then it was the lawyers rather than their own masters whom they suspected as being the cause of their troubles.

We get a glimpse of the life of priests and people in the manual of Canon Myrc, of Shropshire. He wrote a book to instruct and guide his fellow-clergy. It was not very original, a compilation from official sources, but it was a useful popular manual. It contained careful directions for saying Mass and hearing Confessions, with discreet suggestions about what should be done when the penitent was a woman. Among the things which penitents may be told to remember are such faults as leaving gates open for cattle to stray, or walking through a growing crop. The book reveals the author as a faithful priest in a well-ordered parish.

The social organization of medieval life was feudal. There were various ranks of society, with the king at the top. It was not possible to pass from one rank to another. All ranks had duties to those below them, and could claim protection from those above. The only people who could rise higher than their birth warranted were the clergy, because they were of no class. Apart from them all had their assured places, for many a very humble and comfortless place, in the social fabric, but there was a kind of security. No one was ever quite forgotten.

In theory all land belonged to the monarch. The tenants-in-chief, the barons, held from him. They were his 'men', did homage to him, and were bound to fight for him in his wars. From them the smaller tenants held their land, and they were the soldiers of their landlords, as we can see in the Wars of the Roses. At the bottom were the peasants, who had strips of land which they cultivated in the intervals of working on the fields of the lord of the manor or fighting in his battles. The order of serfs or villeins, who were not slaves, but were bound to the soil, and could not transfer their labour to another master, gradually came to an end during this period. The system was possible only because four-fifths of the population were countrymen. One of the things that helped to break feudalism was the rising importance of the towns and of the merchant class. They resented, and sometimes shook off, the power of the baron or the big monastery.

The picture is English, but on the Continent it was much the same, except that in Central Europe it was not the King, but the Emperor, and in France a great noble like the Duke of Burgundy was to all intents a king. One of the effects of feudalism was to curb for a time the rising tide of nationalism. When men began to feel in their bones that they were English or French, the old feudal ties withered.

The Church was organized in the same sort of way. Gregory VII (Hildebrand) was shrewd enough to see what a useful system feudalism was. He would have the Church like that. The ecclesiastics were his men, his soldiers, and the lay-people would take their tone from them. He was the supreme head. The monks and friars, being extra-diocesan, were an even better instrument for him than the secular or parish clergy who owed allegiance to their bishop. It was a great idea, and it did provide a spiritual cement which was much needed in a passionate, hot-blooded age.

The cement was strong, but cracks in the edifice appear in the fourteenth century. In *The Canterbury Tales*, for example, the system is still taken for granted. They are all going on pilgrimage. It is something of a holiday, but they all believe that the journey will earn merit. They are all Churchmen. They mean to live in the Christian faith, and above all they mean to die in it, and, if they can afford it, they will leave money for Masses to be said for them after death, but the poet delicately reveals their weaknesses. Except for the Knight, who is an honourable gentleman, the Plowman, who is an honest fair-dealing, charitable man, and the 'poor' parson of a town, that is, in Chaucer's terminology, a village, who is a humble disciple of his Master, there is something wrong with all of them. The monk and the friar both reveal that they are in the habit of breaking in various ways the rules of their Orders, and neither of them ought really to have been on pilgrimage at all. The wife of Bath is a wealthy old wanton. She has been on all the famous pilgrimages, including the trip to Compostella in honour of St James, but it was more because she wanted to see sights than because she had seen visions. The Abbess is a perfect lady, but her dress is over-fine, and it is her table-manners rather than her piety which are commended. And she also ought not to have been on pilgrimage at all. The summoner and the pardoner are slimy.

These are cracks in the fabric, and there were plenty more. Among the clergy there were abuses like pluralism, non-residence, place-hunting, greedy appetite for fees, ignorance of both Latin and theology. The pages of Langland and Gower are full of all this. And there were sexual delinquencies. Many of the parochial clergy were married. The duty of strict celibacy was proclaimed again and again, especially since Hildebrand, and in England especially by Anselm, but clerical marriage was not uncommon. The marriages were permanent, and, except that they were wholly uncanonical, they were, in a sense, respectable. It was not unknown for son to succeed father in a benefice. The records of diocesan discipline show that there were some clergy who were guilty of more serious sex-offences. Diocesan records naturally reveal the seamy side, as that to which attention had to be called. They do not by themselves give the complete picture. Doubtless, the majority lived simple, innocent lives, but even so there were not many like Gilbert of Sempringham, who in the twelfth century had been a model parish priest. He gave alms to the utmost of his ability, he had a school in his parish in which he himself taught, he was devout, and his people learned from him to be reverent in Church and to be brotherly and charitable in their lives. He founded the one purely English monastic order, the Gilbertines, which at the Dissolution had twenty-five houses.

Among the laity there were, of course, the ordinary sins and failings of men and women. Perhaps the most general defect of the medieval laity was a disposition to be content with a decent minimum of Catholic piety and conduct, and leave everything else to those whose vocation it might be supposed to be, and then to grumble at them if they did not rise to it.

In the fifteenth century the cracks were more visible, and there was not a little anti-clericalism. Not in the parishes, against their own priest, but in general, and especially in relation to the higher clergy. Archdeacons were particularly obnoxious, because their visits were costly and involved the nosing out of offences. Parishioners were as a rule warmly attached to their own priest. They heard Mass regularly, kneeling devoutly at the Elevation, and they performed the substance of what the priest required of them, but the higher clergy had lost the confidence of the people. When Wolsey was tottering to his fall, the Duke of Suffolk, the King's friend and brother-in-law, said publicly, 'it was never merry while we had Cardinals in England'. It was a sign that the day of the great medieval ecclesiastic was over. Men still loved and enriched or rebuilt their parish churches, but there was a tendency for the rich to leave their money to endow colleges rather than to monastic or strictly ecclesiastical objects.

The religious verse of the fifteenth century, often very beautiful, is rather in a minor key, as though the singers were preparing to anoint a body for its burial. Here is a specimen, by John Audeley, a Shropshire monk:

> As I lay sick in my langúre,
>   In an abbey here by west,
> This book I made with great dolóur,
>   When I might not sleep nor rest.
>   Oft with my prayers my soul I blest,
> And said aloud to Heaven's King:
>   I know, O Lord, it is the best,
> Meekly to take thy visiting;
> Else well I wot that I were lorne,
>   High above all lords be He blest,
>   All that thou cost is for the best;
> By fault of thee was no man lost
>   That is here of Woman born.

It was an age full of superstition. Everyone believed in witches, and the religion of many looks like little more than a cultus and a handful of formulas. But there was something more. Religion was over-much preoccupied with thoughts of death, and of what would happen after death. Here again the Church knew. The Church will see that we are all right in the end, if we obey her voice. There is something very solemn about this preoccupation, this fear, and this reassurement. The medieval people really believed in Heaven and Hell. Medieval sermons were about Heaven and Hell. The Morality Plays were about Heaven and Hell. Life was a pilgrimage, and on the way in which it was lived there depended this soul-searching alternative. Now this provides a seriousness which goes far deeper than superstition. It was faith, not very well-reasoned, rather frightened, but sincere.

Many of them did not live as the precepts of the Church demanded that they should. But they all knew that they ought to live like that. Their personal ethics were simple and rather wooden. Sex rather baffled them. They had strong desires, about which they were not silent, like Victorian people, but they were rather ashamed of them. It had been so driven into them that virginity was the perfect condition. Edward the Confessor had been counted as saintly because it was believed that he and his Queen lived like father and daughter. This gave them a distorted view of life. Yet it is surely much that religion made an impression on three regions of human life which are commonly thought rather obstinate, sex, war, and money-making. Husbands and wives were sometimes unfaithful to their vows. But they knew that they ought not to be. They never defended it with cant about self-expression or living your own life. Their wars were cruel and devastating (there are some grim passages in *Henry V*), but religion did have some humanizing effects on war. Their finances were primitive. There was the doctrine of the just price. An egg or a leg of mutton was worth so much, and no more could rightly be asked for it, a doctrine which was later made a little more elastic, as a concession to the existence of different circumstances at different

D 2

times,[1] and it was believed that interest ought not to be exacted, a belief which made useful developments impossible. Yet there is much to be said for a view of life in which charity is the leading virtue and avarice the worst sin. The charity was often indiscriminate and unconstructive, and for avarice it would have been still better if they had substituted pride, but a society which condemns avarice and wishes to be charitable is on one of the roads which lead to the Kingdom.

It was indeed a grand thing that there was a Christendom, a Christian Europe. The one solid gain of the Crusades had been to make Europe conscious of itself as Christian, *vis-à-vis* with Islam. The Crusaders themselves had been anti-Islam, and had in fact failed of their object. But they constructed something which remained, of which we feel the need to-day. Sir Henry Slesser, in his book *Order and Disorder*, a careful examination of Augustinian and Scholastic philosophy, finds it an unhappy defect of modern thought that there are multitudes of counsellors and masses of counsel, but it is all different, and much of it a contradiction of everything else. It is no doubt too late to desire that there should be one philosophy. The search for truth goes where it will and may not be controlled. But to have lost the idea of Christian Europe with agreed principles of thought and life, is to have lost much. There are modern statesmen who are trying manfully to revive the idea of the Christian West, but it is at present, to adapt the famous epigram by Thomas Hobbes, not much more than the ghost of medieval Christendom sitting upon the grave thereof.

From another point of view Mr Middleton Murry regrets the disappearance of the medieval village, where all lived near the soil, and by the soil, when harvest really was harvest, and men knew that if their fields bore well or ill they themselves would be well-fed or hungry in the coming winter. He feels that religion has never recovered from the effects of the betrayal of the poor man by the medieval

1. See R. H. Tawney, *Religion and the Rise of Capitalism*, 40–1.

Church and the de-humanizing process which set in at the Reformation. He sums it up by saying that Christianity succumbed to Nationalism. 'Nowadays the one body of which men are really aware is the nation. That is the unity they know, and feel, and obey.'[1] No Christian who remembers that the Church was built up in the first century in such places as Corinth and Ephesus, can ever quite despair. But it needs more faith and more imagination than is commonly to be had. And in any case those days are gone. The clock of civilization cannot be put back at will.

One brave attempt to arrest the decay was made in the Conciliar movement. Gerson and D'Ailly, and others with them, suggested that the authority of a General Council, if such could be held, would be greater than that of a Pope. Such Councils were held, but it was too late. They were ineffective, and the medieval Church went on to its disaster.

It seems on very many grounds a pity that a culture in many ways so generous and beneficent should come crashing down. But it was already falling by its own weakness, and God seems only to use human eras for as long as they remain useful. When the time comes, He uses something else. The new instrument is doubtless more suited to the time, but, being human, has its imperfections as surely as the old.

1. *The Price of Leadership,* 99.

7

Destruction and Reconstruction

THERE were many causes for what is called the Reformation. There was a general feeling in the sixteenth century that the old standards of measurement were too small. It was a little like the discovery of Relativity. A new continent across the Atlantic had been added to the world, and though no one could calculate, or even guess, to what this would eventually grow, it was clearly a sign that the stage of human action was larger than had been envisaged by the old categories. The Roman eagles had been almost everywhere in Europe, but they had not known America. The thoughts of men were accordingly expanded.

Science was just beginning its conquering career. Roger Bacon, the English friar of the thirteenth century, had been its father, but by this time there were numerous researchers, including Leonardo da Vinci, in the intervals of painting, who were beginning to explore the physical secrets of the universe. And there was before long to be Galileo with his startling reconstruction of the old astronomy.

The new learning was a great contributing cause. The Greek language had quite recently been re-discovered, and the movement known as the Renaissance saw a passion for Greek art, Greek literature, and the Greek way of life. It was not in the South of Europe very wholesome. Many of the Italian Hellenists, including Cardinals and Popes, became paganized and vicious. Not only Socrates but also Alcibiades was among the patron saints of the Italian Renaissance. In Northern Europe it took a healthier form. The Humanists, as the Greek scholars were called, read the New Testament no longer in the Vulgate, but in the original language, and this gave them many new ideas. John Colet, afterwards Dean of St Paul's, lectured at Oxford on St Paul's Epistles not simply as a mine from which proof-texts could be quoted, but as real documents, letters written by a man to men, and made a great sensation. Erasmus edited the first printed New Testament in Greek, and in the intervals of scholarship poked fun at the more vulnerable points of medievalism. At Oxford Bishop Fox and Bishop Oldham founded a College (Corpus Christi) which was to be a stronghold of 'the Greeks' as against the 'Trojans', which was the nickname for those who still clung to the old Latin Scholasticism.

At Cambridge a company of young graduates, which included Thomas Cranmer, used to meet at an inn, which was dubbed Little Germany, to read and discuss the books which were coming in from the Continent. Henry VIII in his young, happy days, before he sank into the morose and bloodthirsty tyrant, was an eager student of the New Learning. Even Wolsey, though he had no time to study it, was in its favour.

The greatest of the English Renaissance men, the fine flower of the remains of medievalism, as it was quickened by the New Learning, was Thomas More. In the end he came down on the Pope's side, because the King was insatiable, and because More could not see how the Catholic Church and the Catholic religion, to which he was devoted, could be maintained without the Pope. Yet he was clearly of the transition period, and it is possible that if he had lived a century later, he might have been on the side of Charles I and Laud.

Another cause was the rising tide of nationalism. In the old feudal days the peasant hardly knew that he was French or English. He was the man of the Duke of Burgundy or the Earl of Warwick. He was for York or Lancaster. In Shaw's *Saint Joan* there is a remarkable dialogue between a Bishop and an Earl, in which each of them delicately suggests to the other that this new sense of nationalism 'may bring you down'. It did not actually do that in either case, but it made a considerable difference to both. In England national feeling had always been stronger than elsewhere, and there was more consciousness of the fact that the Pope was a foreigner than there was in France or Germany or Spain.

To go rather deeper into the causes, the medieval system was wearing out. The Church, both in its general administration and in its central activity, the Mass, had become sadly over-clericalized. What had been intended to be a community of brothers, with its leaders 'taking the oversight, not for filthy lucre, but of a ready mind, neither as being lords over God's heritage, but being examples to the flock', had become an army, with a powerful and well-paid staff, conventionalized regimental officers, and obedient, rather automatic troops. What had been founded to give brothers a perpetual means of communion with their Master and with one another, a thing to be *done*, and to be done by all, had become something *said* by the priest, and heard and looked at by all people.

The level of monastic life had sunk. The monasteries were overbuilt, there were fewer recruits, and the old zeal had waned. There were some scandals, not nearly so many as was alleged in the mass-produced catalogues which served as evidence for the Commissioners who carried out the inquisition, but there were some, and it is certain that in most houses the life had become conventional and rather lazy. The actual motives of Henry VIII's policy were a desire to put one of the Pope's principal weapons out of action, and greed. The dispossessed monks and nuns were for the most part treated fairly enough. The general verdict on the whole business must surely be that something rather drastic needed to be done, but that the total abolition of the religious life in England was spiritually, intellectually, and socially, a loss. It was unpopular with the English people, and in the North it led to a serious insurrection, the Pilgrimage of Grace.

In the religion of the people there had come to be too much fear, and too much superstition. Death and its terrors loomed very large in their imaginations. The old, happy confidence with which the early Christians laid their dead to rest had been replaced by terrified forebodings, palliated only by the existence of an insurance system, with premiums that were rather high for the pockets of the poor. Pilgrimages had had their day. Relics were beginning to be sniffed at. The Mass was still intensely sacred, but it was valued because it enabled the congregation 'to see God', a description of Christian worship which those modern Christians who would not regard it as wholly false would certainly not receive as the whole truth. The fact is that religion had become mechanical.

The thing that precipitated the movement on the Continent was Luther's indignation at the sale of Indulgences up and down the country by travelling pardoners. Behind that was his discovery of the Pauline teaching that man is justified by faith, that is, a right relation to Christ, rather than by the performance of works. The thing which had precipitated the breach with Rome in England was the King's wish for a son and heir. Katharine's children, except Mary, had all died. He fell in love with Anne, who would not have him except as Queen, and in any case he wanted a prince. He may quite possibly have had scruples about having married his brother Arthur's widow. Anyhow, he wanted his marriage to be dissolved. It was not to be a divorce, but a declaration that the marriage had been from the beginning null and void. The Pope would no doubt have given such a declaration, but he was at the time in the power of the Emperor, who was Katharine's nephew. He temporized, and finally refused, and that brought Wolsey, the great Cardinal, down. The King, having carefully trained Parliament to be his instrument, shook off the Pope, dissolved the monasteries, and broke the power of the clergy, but there was in his reign not much doctrinal change. Henry's ideal was a non-papal, national, King-ruled Catholicism.

The English people took the abolition of papal jurisdiction without a murmur. The English are like that, caring more about things that affect their daily lives than about large principles. They were for the most part rather glad that the clergy had received a set-back, but sorry about the monasteries. Materially, they gained nothing. The land was not given back to them, and the new landlords were harder than the old.

It is never possible to abolish an old-standing thing, or even seriously to curtail its influence, without putting something in its place. This need was supplied by the Bible. The main outlines of the Bible-story had been made known to the rank and file by means of church-windows, miracle plays, and such sermons as there were. Men came to know something of Adam, Noah, Abraham, Moses, David and so forth, and of the Nativity, Passion, and Resurrection of our Lord. The educated knew Latin and could read the Bible in the Vulgate. The Vulgate was a definitely Catholic translation, and in places tendentious. Thus for the word now translated 'repent' the Vulgate said *agere poenitentiam*, 'do penance' (e.g. Acts ii, 38; xvii, 30). The discovery of the New Testament made people rub their eyes and say, 'But this is very different from what the Church says and does.'

Of course it was at first very crudely interpreted. Tyndale and many of the new Bible students and translators were thoroughly anti-Church. They added to their versions annotation which was strongly and often virulently Protestant, and they suggested that everything which was not expressly ordered in the New Testament was therefore wrong. They were also wholly uncritical. The Bible was the Word of God and all parts of it, except, of course, the ceremonial laws of the Old Testament, were of equal value. It was a hastily-grasped weapon to put in place of the Church. In course of time it came to be understood that the Church was still, as it had always been, the teaching authority, and that its Bible, the greatest of its possessions, was the standard by which developments could and should be checked. In the beginning it was used by the more ardent reformer as a club with which to beat the Church.

In England the Reformation took a long time; about a hundred and thirty years. The short reign of Edward VI saw a rapidly increasing movement in the Protestant direction. The first English Prayer Book in 1549 was not popular, and its introduction was resisted, especially in Devon and Cornwall. It was liturgically conservative, but it was definitely a reformed Book. The Second Book of 1552 went much further, and represents the extreme limit to which the Church of England ever went in that direction. A few months after its publication the young King died, and the five years of Mary's reign brought back the Pope and medievalism, and introduced Spanish ecclesiastics and Spanish methods of procuring orthodoxy into England. Those five years made it for ever impossible for England to be papal in the old sense.

Elizabeth seems to have inherited a good deal of her father's point of view, but she had a difficult team to drive. The bishoprics were nearly all vacant. Of those bishops who were living only two consented to carry on. The Lower Houses of the Marian Convocations, which were still sitting, were hostile. The returning exiles were hot Puritans, and they at that time had no thought of leaving the Church of England. They held on, and hoped to shape the Church to their pattern. Mary of Scotland was a problem. There were plots against the Queen, which were engineered from abroad. It was, to say the least, not easy for those who were faithful to the old order, who must now be called, for the first time, Roman Catholics, to disassociate their religious allegiance from disloyalty to the Queen. The Queen and her advisers did not help them by their policy, and the Pope finally made things extremely difficult for them by excommunicating the Queen and denouncing her as illegitimate.

What is called the Elizabethan Settlement was very much of a compromise. The Queen was determined to keep a tight hand on the Church and give to it a uniform character, but her policy was monarchical rather than what is commonly called Erastian. She would not allow the Church to be controlled by Parliament, and expected the Bishops and the Convocations to carry out her wishes in a constitutional way. It was fortunate that she had in her kingdom a Christian thinker so profound and so reasonable as Richard Hooker. Hooker was a Church and Queen man, who assumed that Church and Nation were conterminous, but he was also a learned theologian, who thought out the Anglican position from the beginning.

It is sometimes lightly said that under Elizabeth a new Church began. There is in fact no point at which it could truly be said that this happened. When Cardinal Pole died at about the same time as Queen Mary, great pains were taken to ensure that Matthew Parker should be in all respects, ecclesiastical and legal, his lawful successor. On the larger scale, it is incontestable that in the parishes in the times of both Edward VI and Elizabeth the same clergy, the same churchwardens, the same people went on using the Parish Church. The difference was that from 1549 to 1553, and from 1558 onwards, they had English services, and were encouraged to entertain rather different theological ideas.

Under the Stuart Kings the Book of Common Prayer, which Puritan opposition had rather put out of action, came into its own. There was still Puritan opposition, but it was becoming more openly hostile, more obviously separate from the Church. The Roman Catholic Recusants, as they were called, no longer treated as non-conforming members of the one all-inclusive Church of England, were settling down as a community. The great achievement of the reign of James I was the Authorized Version of the Bible, which almost instantly displaced all previous versions and has remained ever since the greatest possession of the English-speaking peoples. Charles I was a thorough Anglican and the Laudian policy was to stiffen up Church discipline, but the influence of the Queen made the position of the Roman Catholics easier.

Then came the Civil War. The Puritans could bear Archbishop Laud's regime no longer, and Parliament was angered by the King's absolute government. In the war the Parliamentary armies were victorious, and the King was eventually a prisoner. Cromwell, for the most part a cautious, prudent man, could not see what could be done with him, and in a rash moment consented to his execution. It was illegal, because the court had no authority, and it was a political mistake, because it rallied English feeling to the martyr's side. The King was very far from faultless as a king, but he was genuinely a martyr for the cause of Church and King.

For eleven years the Church of England was proscribed. The clergy were turned out of their benefices, and the use of the Book of Common Prayer was forbidden. It was used only in holes and corners. The official worship was either Presbyterian or Independent.

By 1661 the English people had had enough of it. Cromwell died, and General Monk and the Presbyterians brought back King Charles II. There was a new Prayer Book and the long course of the English Reformation ended. There have been many reforms since then, and the face of England and the face of English Christianity has changed greatly, but there has been no single large-scale movement which could be called a second Reformation.

The Anglican Church was now top dog, and took full advantage of it. There was at that time in all quarters a passion for uniformity, and not much toleration. The new Prayer Book took it for granted that everyone would be baptized, confirmed, and a communicant, and that public worship would everywhere be on the lines laid down in the Book. In fact the course of events was quite different. The passion for uniformity produced Nonconformity on a large scale. Of the existing ministers, who had been put into their benefices during the Cromwell period, some two thousand were unable to assent to the new Book, and resigned their charges. They were in fact Puritans, quite out of sympathy with Anglican ideals, and it was perhaps impossible to expect anything else, but they were willing to suffer for their principles. Most of them procured preaching-places of some kind, and in this way Nonconformity in England began. The harrying of these Dissenters, which was carried out by means of the Test Act, the Conventicle Act, the Five Mile Act and so forth, was the work not of the Church in Convocation, but of Parliament. The House of Commons was full of country squires, churchmen who had suffered with their clergy during the Cromwell period, and they were determined to assert their rights. From this time began the alliance of squire and parson which has been sometimes beneficial, often a disaster, and has now disappeared. The Bishops had been very overbearing at the Savoy Conference which preceded the making of the new Prayer Book. It is quite arguable that the Puritans were too far off for the Bishops to meet them half way, but the Bishops made no step at all in their direction. From that time there were three kinds of Christianity in England. The story is no longer single and continuous.

The story of the Roman Catholics in England since then stands rather apart from the main stream of English religious life. On the Continent the Reformation was followed by the Counter-Reformation, an invigorating and spiritualizing movement which renewed the vitality of the Church in France, Spain and Italy. The Council of Trent was a reforming Council, and the seventeenth century saw much devoted and successful missionary work by Jesuits and other Roman Catholic evangelists. In this vital matter they were at that time far ahead of the Anglicans and the Puritans. The English Roman Catholics had their heroes and their martyrs, and of course they shared in the quickening effect of the Counter-Reformation. But, except in the North, at that time the less populous and less influential part of the country, they were not numerous. They did not long continue to be thought of as Recusants, rebels to be fined or imprisoned as seditious, as they had often been under

Elizabeth. Nor did they continue to deserve even such part
of the political opprobrium as their forefathers may have
deserved. They in fact disassociated themselves for the most
part from political projects, and lived their own life in
seclusion, but they did not enjoy full citizenship, and were
for a long time a small and unimportant community. In
later centuries they were to be tardily emancipated from
their political disabilities, and grew to be a more influential
part of English religious life.

The Nonconformists, or, as they used to be called, Dissenters, had a difficult existence. They were excluded from
civil office, from degrees at the Universities and from a large
part of English social life. They had their old Puritan
virtues of determination and perseverance, and they
gradually built up a strong organization. They had no
endowments and the whole cost of maintaining their
churches and their ministers came out of their not very well-
filled pockets. In country places they suffered a good deal
from the snobbery of the squire and his circle, and the
Rector as a rule did little to make their lot more pleasant.
In the towns their virility and their independence of social
conventions made their form of religion acceptable to many
of what used to be called the lower middle classes, and they
became a numerous, well-organized, self-supporting community. To fill their chapels, the ministers depended on
good preaching, and the standard of preaching in the chapel
was higher than in the Church. Their theology was Calvin-
istic, and the exposition of the Bible what would now be
called Fundamentalist. There were at first only Indepen-
dents (i.e. Congregationalists) and Baptists, and a few
English Presbyterians. Many of the last named, rather
surprisingly when the orthodox quality of Scottish Presby-
terianism is borne in mind, gradually passed into Unita-
rianism. Methodism did not appear till the eighteenth
century.

The great contribution that Nonconformists have made
to English life has been their devotion to freedom. Exercising

strict discipline within their own circles, and exhibiting, in what used to be called the Nonconformist conscience, an occasional touch of censoriousness, they have passed the torch of freedom from one generation to another. Anglicans, resting on the privileges which were theirs from the seventeenth to the nineteenth century, have often been content to *laisser faire*. 'There are scandals and abuses, no doubt. There will always be such things. It can't be helped.' Free Churchmen have determined to abolish them. Sometimes it was only a restriction by which they were themselves incommoded, but sometimes, as in the case of the old Bulgarian or Armenian 'atrocities', it was an occasion for pure righteous indignation, with no sort of axe to grind. If in some directions the power of Nonconformists, as a separate force, has waned, it is in part at least because its principles, like those of political Liberalism, have permeated all parties, and are no longer the exclusive possession of the body which first exhibited and commended them.

8

Secularization

THE process of secularization operated in two ways:

I. About the middle of the seventeenth century a remarkable intellectual revolution took place in the mind of
England, and indeed of most of Europe. J. N. Figgis, a
shrewd and learned historian of thought, has described it as
the most momentous of the intellectual changes which
ushered in the modern world. It was the secularization of
politics. The Reformers themselves were partly the cause of
this, though it came without their knowledge or intention
and was contrary to their highest principles.

Hitherto religion and politics had been so closely inter-
twined as almost to seem one. In the Middle Ages it was not
only that ecclesiastics discharged the great offices of state
and were Ambassadors, Lord Chancellors, Lord Treasurers,
and what not. It was almost that the Church was totalitarian, and the State was part of it, the officer of the Church
on the secular side. The sort of feeling that a modern ruler
might have when he goes to church, that he is after all only
one of God's people, was present in the mind of a medieval
king all the time, when he went to war, or concluded a
treaty. His royal acts were part of his religion. Medieval
kings committed many crimes. There was plenty of lying
and cheating and cruelty and oppression, but, whereas a
modern government, embarking on a war of aggression,
would hatch up some pretext like the ill-treatment of
Sudeten Germans in Czechoslovakia, medieval rulers
argued about their policies in the language of religion. They
tried to cover their crimes with a cloak of piety. When they
could not pretend even to themselves that they were right,
they had a bad conscience about it. Machiavelli was the

first person to argue seriously that it did not matter. And, apart from what monarchs did, the solution of social and economic problems, land, the use of capital, and so forth, had a religious basis.

In the seventeenth century, Archbishop Laud, entirely accepting the Reformation so far as it had gone, and, indeed, supposing for his part that it was finished, still did his best to maintain the old relations of Church and State. He was Archbishop, zealous in performing his Church functions and promoting obedience to the rubrics and the canons, but he considered it an essential part of his duty to preside over the Court of Star Chamber and to pass judgement upon offenders. He believed that he was preaching the Gospel there as truly as in the pulpit. In a sense, it may actually have been so, because the Courts of Star Chamber and High Commission had jurisdiction over moral offenders, who could not always be brought before the ordinary judges. Laud indeed incurred much unpopularity because he sharply condemned seducers and adulterers and land-enclosers of high social position. Mr R. H. Tawney has shown, too, that the Puritan Richard Baxter took the same medieval view of the interdependence of secular and sacred. He says of Baxter's *Christian Directory* that

it is, in essence, a Puritan *Summa Theologica* and *Summa Moralis* in one; its method of treatment descends directly from that of the mediaeval *Summae*, and it is, perhaps, the last important English specimen of a famous *genus*. ... Divided into four parts, Ethics, Economics, Ecclesiastics and Politics, it has as its purpose to establish the rules of a Christian casuistry, which may be sufficiently detailed and precise to afford practical guidance to the proper conduct of men in the different relations of life, as lawyer, physician, schoolmaster, soldier, master and servant, buyer and seller, landlord and tenant, lender and borrower, ruler and subject. Part of its material is derived from the treatment of similar subjects by previous writers, both before and after the Reformation, and Baxter is conscious of continuity and great tradition.[1]

1. *Religion and the Rise of Capitalism*, 220.

These were high-minded attempts, but the time for such programmes had gone by. From now on religion and theology were going to be regarded as departments of life and knowledge, of greater or less importance, according to taste, but not thought of, even by their exponents, as being in control of public policy.

Religion went, so to speak, into private life. Not till the appearance of the Christian Socialists in the nineteenth century do we find religion claiming to rule all social practice, and even then it was counsel, preaching, argument, an appeal to principle. Any claim to other than moral authority would have been instantly rejected, even if it had been desired to make it. Such 'interference' as was attempted was contemptuously resented by politicians of the Lord Melbourne type.

From the time of Laud and Baxter onwards the point of view changed rapidly. The old interpretation of life had restricted commercial development at many points because it forbade usury. Rent had been thought legitimate, and profits from a business carried on, but interest in the strict sense, a fixed return year by year for capital lent, was frowned upon. It must be remembered that borrowing had meant as a rule borrowing by the poor man in difficulties from the rich man. The modern custom by which nations, municipalities, and corporations borrow large sums, and the resulting capital makes possible large works of production, was unknown. The prohibition of usury had been in the interests of the poor man. Finance in the modern sense, at least within the limits of the nation, was thus impossible for Christian men, and it was accordingly left to the Jews, some of whom had amassed, and rather precariously held, large fortunes. Towards the end of the medieval period international finance began to assert itself among Gentiles. The Fugger family of Augsburg became great capitalists in the fifteenth century. They lent money to the Emperor Charles V, and received commercial concessions in return. They were strict Catholics, and they did it all within the limits allowed or winked at by the Church, but it was the beginning of modern business. The Caursins of Cahors in the South of France, and the Lombardy bankers, who gave their name to Lombard Street in London, were taking the place that had been occupied by the Jews, and the English Guilds were amassing capital, which could be lent to kings and nobles. Church authorities, Popes and Cathedral Chapters, did not scruple to use the resources of capitalist groups.

To this new class of business men Calvinism was congenial. It bade them organize their private lives strictly, but it left them free to expand commercially. It was not that they countenanced any kind of dishonesty or sharp practice. They were scrupulously honest, but they assumed, in a way that had not been known in the Middle Ages, that the world of commerce was one which Christian people need have no hesitation in entering, and prospering therein. Gain became respectable. In this way there gradually grew up the theory, not often put into words, but underlying much social practice, that attention to business will always bring its due reward, and that the poor man is not the natural, God-given object of charity but is reaping the fruits of his own idleness and improvidence. 'God helps those who help themselves' can be a wholesome incentive to co-operation with the divine purpose, but it can also be a hard, and, in effect, ungodly maxim. Calvinism was itself the opposite of *laisser-faire*. It was the strictest of strict disciplines. But one of its results was the genesis of an unsound social theory. In seventeenth-century England, during the short period when the Puritans were in control, and indeed all the time while they had still hoped some day to be in control, they concerned themselves with what they believed to be the Christian idea of Government. But as soon as the Restoration put them in the position of an uninfluential minority, they developed an anti-political complex. Of Herbert Spencer, who was born in 1820 into what he called a family of 'ingrained Nonconformity', a writer in *Blackwood* (January, 1904) wrote:

The Nonconformist of 1662, who survived till the Education Act of 1870 made him a solecism, held that Government conducted on worldly principles – any kind of Government, excepting a Theocracy, or rule of the saints – was a thing with which no Christian could have anything to do; the principle of Government was constraint; the principle of Christian life was voluntary obedience; to the consistent Nonconformist Government was a *sin*.

There is a certain pitiful irony in the fact that the Puritans, who of all Englishmen were the most eager to rule every thought and action by their religion, should have paved the way to the secularization of a large area of human life. But it was so, at least for a time. The political Nonconformity of the nineteenth century (on the Liberal side) was a later growth, and not the same thing. It was within the accepted, conventional range of contemporary party politics. The Church mostly voted Conservative, and the Nonconformists, almost to a man, voted Liberal. Even this is sometimes thought to have been, on both sides, a secularization of religion rather than a sanctification of politics.

It was not merely that the assumptions and ordinary practice of politicians came to be based on a secular view of life. Political science itself became secular. Religious considerations were set apart on a sideboard. Hooker had written nobly about law, that 'of her there can be no less acknowledged than that her seat is the bosom of God, her voice the harmony of the world: all things in heaven and earth do her homage, the very least as feeling her care, and the greatest as not exempted from her power.' Hooker was a Church and Queen man, and in his day it was still possible to say that Church and Nation consisted of the same people, an identification which was less accurate in the time of Burke, and still less when Dr Arnold and Dean Stanley reasserted it in the nineteenth century. The philosophical mantle of Hooker fell on Locke (1632–1704), who, though a religious man and a Christian, reasoned about questions of philosophy and epistemology as purely intellectual problems. Hooker was not a medievalist. He had been a pioneer in preparing the approach to reality which Anglicanism, released from its captivity to scholastic postulates, was gradually to make. He argued that Christian faith and thought rested on the threefold basis of the Church, the Bible, and Reason. He blazed the trail for Churchmen, but not for philosophy in general. Locke had a great reverence for the Bible, and some regard for the Church, if it were not too dogmatic, but he rested his case on reason. He led the way to the secularization of political and other science. Further, the scientific discoveries of Newton and others in the nineteenth century, though the scientists were for the most part profoundly religious men, helped to produce an atmosphere in which Locke's personal religion was forgotten and his rationalizing was remembered and extended. The eighteenth century was called the Age of Reason.

The *Zeitgeist* in that century produced the Deists. Some of them were nominally Christians, but they argued that Christianity was 'not mysterious' and was in fact the religion of all reasonable men. Others, not calling themselves Christians, were content to believe in a God who had created the world, and thereafter had retired into inactivity, with no occupation beyond the contemplation of the perfection of His own handiwork. Against this Bishop Butler brought to bear the heavy artillery of his precise reasoning. He scored an overwhelming victory, and made Deism for ever an impossible creed. When Butler is reproached for not having done more than he did, it must be remembered that he did the whole of what he set out to do.

Another answer to the freezing tendency of the Deists and the Latitudinarians came from the mystics. William Law, a disciple of Jacob Boehme, wrote powerfully and persuasively. His *Serious Call* had a converting appeal on many, including Samuel Johnson, and his other more general theological writings had an illuminating effect. John Wesley, of whom more presently, preached a more emotional religion than was fashionable in his day, and the hymn-writers, Charles Wesley, William Cowper, and John Newton, had their appeal in a region which the conventional religion of the period hardly touched.

II. This leads to the second element in the secularizing process, the secularization of the Church itself. The Church of England under Charles II had a great opportunity. It is hardly too much to say that it was thrown away with both hands. It is true that the Caroline divines produced massive, learned and well-thought-out theology, which has become in a rather academic sense classical. That is to say, no one reads it, but it is of fine, solid, enduring quality. And there were laymen like Evelyn, Boyle, and Sir Thomas Browne, who were both cultured and devout. It is also true that when James II tried to staff the universities with Roman Catholics, and defied the law in his attempt to Romanize the country, the Church made a spirited protest, which was very popular. The acquittal of the Seven Bishops, who had protested against the high-handed action of the King, was the last time in English history when the Bishops were popular heroes. It is a little humiliating that it is often much easier to incur popularity by standing against something than by standing for something. Yet in a true sense it may be said that the Seven Bishops stood for the Law of England, as it then was.

It cannot be pretended that the Church made a good use of its dominating position after the Restoration. The passion for uniformity which prevailed at that time made Churchmen want to bind all Englishmen into the Prayer Book mould, and their relief at having escaped from the chains of the Cromwell period made them proud and intolerant.

Moreover, at the accession of Dutch William the Church of England suffered a great loss. Several bishops, and some hundreds of the other clergy, having taken the oath of allegiance to King James, did not feel that the action of Parliament in making William and Mary King and Queen absolved them from it. They were not Romanizers, they were not Jacobites in the sense of the Scottish risings of '15 and '45, but they had sworn an oath and they could not forget it. They resigned their benefices and went out into private life. Many of the laity followed them, and thus the Church lost much of its best material. The Non-Jurors, as they were called, worshipped apart for a time, and indeed constructed for themselves a Prayer Book which was more faithful to primitive models than the official Book of 1662, but in course of time the sect dwindled and died.

It was not that all who remained were conscienceless time-servers, but it is the fact that from that time the Church began to acquire a new character. In place of the Catholic theology and the rotund rhetoric of the Caroline divines, congregations now heard reasoned discourses, setting forth at very considerable length the grounds for orthodox belief and the rationality of Christian ethics. There were among the preachers men of lofty moral tone like Tillotson and South, but there were also some who were content to occupy lower ground. Thus Bishop Warburton offered the following singular explanation of the assumed diminution of the Pentecostal Gifts:

A further reason for the abatement of the influence of the supporting spirit of grace is the peace and security of the Church. There was a time when the powers of the world were combined together for its destruction. At such a period nothing but aid from above could support humanity in sustaining such a conflict as that which the holy martyrs encountered with joy and rapture, the horrors of death in torment. But now the profession of the Christian faith is attended with ease and honour; and the conviction, which the weight of human testimony and the conclusions of human reason, afford us of its truth, is abundantly sufficient to support us in our religious perseverance.

There had been a revival under Queen Anne. She was a staunch Churchwoman, who generously remitted a large sum of money which had been appropriated by the Crown ever since the days of the grasping Queen Elizabeth. It had come from the first-fruits of benefices, and it was now formed into the Church fund known, until it was quite recently merged into the general fund of the Church Commissioners, as Queen Anne's Bounty. In her reign there was a revival of churchmanship, and the Society for Promoting Christian Knowledge and the Society for the Propagation of the Gospel in Foreign Parts were both founded.

Under the Georges came a sad relapse. George I was a German, knowing nothing of England or the English Church. He conformed (John and James II are the only English Kings who did not receive Holy Communion at their Coronations), but he was not interested. Nor was his successor. During the eighteenth century England was governed by the great Whig families. Walpole was Prime Minister from 1715 to 1717 and 1721 to 1742. He appointed Whig bishops, the younger sons of the great families, or scholars who had been tutors to a young Duke or Earl. They were respectable, not unbelieving, like some of the French high ecclesiastics, but they had no zeal. In fact, 'enthusiasm', which at that time meant what we call fanaticism, was the thing that most frightened them. They conceived it their duty to remain in London during the winter months, attending at the House of Lords, voting for Government measures and speaking only when the supposed 'interests of the Church' were involved. During the summer months they visited their dioceses, and confirmed and performed other episcopal duties very diligently. The Bishop of Exeter, for example, visited South Devon in one summer, North Devon in the next, and Cornwall in the third.

None of them, not even Butler with his grave intellectual power, nor Wake with his interest in the Eastern Church, nor Gibson with his exceptional knowledge of the Canon Law, nor Berkeley with his Idealist philosophy, pious and conscientious as they were, reached either the primitive or the modern standard for a bishop. They were not, except Wilson in the remote Isle of Man, first and foremost shepherds of the flock.

One of the things which helped to make the Church ineffective in this century was the fact that the bishops were the sole representatives of the Church in public life. Convocation, the ancient Parliament of the Church, was suppressed from 1717 to 1852. The lower Houses had resented the Erastian utterances of Bishop Hoadley, who by dint of judicious self-adaptation to his environment, was Bishop successively of Bangor, Hereford, Salisbury, and Winchester. They were thought to be Jacobites in their sympathies, as indeed most of them were, though not to the point of actual rebellion, and they were suppressed. The result was that the only spokesmen of the Church were the Whig Bishops in the House of Lords.

Some voices were raised against the prevailing influence. The Three Letters of William Law to the Bishop of Bangor (Hoadley) are a masterpiece of wit and churchmanship. Hoadley was perfectly willing to confirm and ordain, because that was the required thing, but he had little belief in the spiritual efficacy of what he did. Law searchingly exposed the barren poverty of his position.

Another voice, more widely heard, was that of John Wesley. Wesley, whose life was almost conterminous with the century, was the bright light of it. He was actually all his life an Anglican churchman. The name of Methodist was originally given to him and his undergraduate friends at Oxford because of their scrupulous adherence to the rubrics and provisions of the Prayer Book. He experienced what was called a sensible conversion and he began a roving ministry which was too large for the Church of the period. He chafed against restrictions, and preached everywhere and to everyone, in fields, at pit-heads, at street corners. He aroused Englishmen wherever he went – and his journeys were incessant – to a great pitch of enthusiastic and sometimes rather queer excitement. Everywhere he formed his disciples into classes, with local class-leaders. He did not intend that they should be in any sense schismatic. They were to attend the Parish Church on Sunday mornings, and on Sunday evenings and at other times they were to meet elsewhere for the worship of God and mutual edification. He himself, though he committed an ecclesiastical irregularity in laying hands on Dr Coke, lived and died a Churchman, but it was almost inevitable that the Methodists should break away, as they did. A medieval Pope had been wise enough to see that Francis and his friars were to be encouraged, but the horizons of the eighteenth-century English bishops were too limited to entertain the Methodists. Yet they have remained the nearest of all the non-Anglican sects to the Mother Church.

The value of the work of John Wesley is quite incalculable. He was the one really burning and shining light in a dark period. Historians have described him as the man who saved England, or as the man who ensured that the French Revolution did not also happen here, and that the Labour movement, when it subsequently came, was not anti-Christian. The Methodists learned something of what may be called political methods in the management of their local classes, and many of the early Labour politicians were Methodist class-leaders.

The Church of England was at that time too stuffy to breathe the atmosphere which he created. 'Sir', said one of the best of the bishops of the period, 'this pretending to special gifts of the Holy Ghost is a very horrid thing.' Whitefield, his great colleague, the man of whom David Garrick said, 'I would give a hundred pounds to be able to say "Oh" as Mr Whitefield says it,' was a Calvinist. Wesley was of the other, or Arminian, school of thought. His preaching was at times what would now be thought overemotional, but it touched the conscience of England, and the hymns of his brother Charles had an even wider and more permanent appeal. They include 'Hark! the herald angels sing', 'Let saints on earth' and 'Jesu, lover of my soul.'

9

Revival

In the latter part of the eighteenth and the earlier part of the nineteenth century there occurred what is called the Evangelical Revival. Methodism was a large part of it, but part of it came strictly within the limits of the Church of England. The Evangelicals have two great achievements to their credit. The first was that they abolished slavery. The Friends, always foremost in every unpopular good cause, had been the first to take it up, but the group of Church of England Evangelicals known as the Clapham Sect carried it through. William Wilberforce was their spokesman in Parliament, Venn was the Rector of Clapham, Thornton, the rich and generous banker, was their chief financial supporter, Clarkson, Granville Sharp, and Teignmouth Shore were among the devoted workers for the cause, and behind it all were the selfless, lifelong labours – always, if possible, anonymous – of Zachary Macaulay. It took them a long time. There was much prejudice against them, in which Lord Nelson shared, and there was the profit-motive of the slave-traders to contend with. Parliament was at first uninterested, then unwilling, and only by slow degrees was the majority obtained. Pitt, who agreed with them, would not make it a Government matter, and it was not till 1807 that the slave trade was made illegal. This was not final victory. In 1833 slavery in the British Dominions was wholly abolished. This was a real victory. The British taxpayer put his hand into his pocket to the tune of twenty millions, to compensate the owners. Lecky describes the Act of 1807 as one of the three or four perfectly virtuous acts recorded in the history of nations. Wilberforce did not live to see the final victory. His place as leader of the group had now been taken by Sir Thomas Fowell Buxton.

The other great achievement was the re-creation of the missionary spirit in the minds of English Churchmen. In early days the English Church had been very missionary-hearted. Themselves the fruit of foreign missions, they were eager to hand on the torch, and it is only one example of their zeal that Winfrid, called Boniface, went from Devon to be the Apostle of Germany. In the Middle Ages European Christians were content to think that there was a Christian Europe, and gave little thought to Asia or Africa, though Francis of Assisi knew that evangelism was better than Crusades and Raymond Lully in the fourteenth century made an eager but unsuccessful attempt to found missionary colleges to send preachers to the Moslem world. The Reformation was so exacting a period that the necessity of missionary work was almost forgotten. The Counter-Reformation on the Continent, especially in France, produced many devoted workers overseas, and Spanish missionaries converted large areas in South America, but in England the anxieties of the Reformation and the complacence of the eighteenth century had the effect of killing evangelistic zeal. The Society for the Propagation of the Gospel had indeed been founded in 1701, but for long it was a small affair, and was chiefly concerned with ministering to white people abroad. This was, of course, a vital work, and there are vigorous parishes to-day in the United States which look back with pride to their foundation by S.P.G. two hundred years ago, but not much was done by Englishmen for the heathen. The Church Missionary Society was founded by the Evangelicals in 1799, to evangelize Africa and the East, and has ever since been a powerful spiritual instrument of the Christian cause in the world. No one who has not to some extent been inside it can understand the affection with which 'the old C.M.S.' is regarded in many an English parish, and there are millions of coloured people, perhaps above all in Uganda, who owe to it the free, peaceful, and happy conditions in which they now live and, as St Paul puts it, 'Yea, and their own souls also.'

These two achievements of the Evangelicals are the more remarkable because in other respects it was a defect of their quality to be rather over-individualist. There were, for example, gaps in Wilberforce's social policy. He was disposed for the most part to say that the poor should be contented with their lot, and that, if they were good, they would be compensated for their hardships in the after-life. As a compassionate man, he regretted the bloodshed of Peterloo, but did not see what else could have been done. This caused William Cobbett to dislike him very much. To Hannah More, who was genuinely concerned for the welfare of the miners in the Mendip Hills, it never occurred that higher wages or better conditions were among the objects which Christian people should try to secure for their ill-paid and uncomfortably-housed neighbours.

This was, of course, a defect. Many of them were in fact far better than their creed. Lord Shaftesbury in the nineteenth century, himself a believer in personal conversion as the one thing needful, nevertheless worked untiringly to improve the conditions of sweeps' boys and other oppressed persons. Yet he was never a whole-hearted believer in education, nor did he as a social reformer penetrate to causes.

Within the personal sphere the Evangelicals wrought a great change in English life. Much that was devilish in the morals of the rich, and much that was beastly in the manners of the poor, disappeared before their conscience-searching appeals. It may be that they spoke of Christ overmuch as the Deliverer from the wrath to come, and it may be that they were rather obsessed with thoughts of judgement and hell, but they did proclaim Christ and the necessity of personal conversion, and conversion, on their lips, implied a very high standard of life. The Evangelical leaders were men of steadfast, noble character. Each hour of time, each pound of money, was to be accounted for.

They worked, and prayed, and gave their charitable gifts 'as in the great Taskmaster's eye'.

Not of the Clapham Sect, but of the Evangelicals, was William Cowper. He was the friend of John Newton, the converted slave-dealer. It has been sometimes said that Newton's Calvinism drove Cowper into his occasional fits of madness. Chesterton, for instance, remarked that Cowper was almost damned by John Calvin, and saved by John Gilpin. A modern critic, Lord David Cecil, concludes that his religion was not the cause of his madness.

Meantime, in the parishes, such men as Romaine, Fletcher of Madeley, Venn of Huddersfield, Grimshaw, and, above all, Charles Simeon at Cambridge, were building up a strong religion. An attractive picture of it can be seen in George Eliot's *Scenes from Clerical Life*, or, so far as Methodism is concerned, in *Adam Bede*. The Anglican Evangelicals were stout Churchmen, using the Prayer Book faithfully, though not quite in its entirety, and their not very frequent Communion services were attended by very large numbers of very earnest worshippers.

The Evangelicals were not popular. They were thought to be straight-laced and puritanical. Patrons of benefices did not appoint them, and it was for this reason that the Simeon Trust was founded, to buy advowsons and secure the appointment of Evangelical incumbents. The purchase of advowsons is not in itself a good thing, and it has since been made impossible, but at the time it seemed to the Evangelicals the only way.

Many tributes could be quoted to the good life and good example of the Evangelicals. It will suffice to remember the words of Mr Gladstone:

The Evangelical clergy were the heralds of a real and profound revival, the revival of spiritual life. Every Christian under their scheme had personal dealing with his Lord and Saviour.

That was their secret. They were eager at all times to keep open the door which gave them access to a personal Saviour.

It may be that they reiterated overmuch the challenge, 'Choose ye this day whom ye will serve', that they were over-fond of saying 'Decide, decide to-night', but their own decision, once made, was steadfastly maintained.

The second revival was at the time known as the Oxford Movement. It is now generally spoken of as the Catholic Revival. Among its precursors were Coleridge, who perceived the necessity of the Catholic Church, and Sir Walter Scott, who brought before his readers the romance of the Middle Ages. It was in the main a re-assertion of the ideas of the seventeenth century Caroline divines, Pearson, Taylor, Beveridge, Bull, Thorndike, especially as they had lately been re-interpreted by Jebb, an Irish Bishop, and a layman, Alexander Knox. Keble began the movement in England with his famous Assize Sermon on National Apostasy in 1833. Newman soon joined him, and inaugurated the series of *Tracts for the Times*, which gave the party for a time the name of Tractarians. The Tracts, which were at first short pamphlets, developed, especially when Pusey joined Newman and Keble, into long treatises with catenas of quotations from Patristic and Caroline divines. Their main object was to assert that the Church of England was a true part of the Catholic Church, the Body of Christ. The State had not made it, and the State could not destroy it. The early leaders of the movement were not what is commonly called ritualists (the proper term is 'ceremonialist'), and they made no change in the manner of conducting services or in the furnishings of the Church. Only they reaffirmed with intense earnestness the God-given authority of the Church. It was the thing needful to fill the gap left in the teaching of the Evangelicals.

By degrees suspicion was aroused. Pusey's teaching about the Real Presence of Christ in the Eucharist, and about priestly absolution, gave offence to many. Newman, challenged to say what he made of the Thirty-nine Articles, always regarded as the bulwark of Anglican Protestantism, showed that they were 'patient of a Catholic interpretation', as indeed they were, having been intended as comprehensive articles of peace. This, at the time, was thought disingenuous, and Newman was denounced by Bishops as disloyal. He had already had his moments of uneasiness about his position in the Church of England, but this settled it. He took a long time to consider it, but he was gradually moving towards the conviction that the Church of England, as a mother, was unable to bring up the children to whom she had given birth, and that his own hope of salvation lay only in the Church of Rome. He was received into it in 1845.

This, and a further crisis which arose in 1850 over a high-handed pronouncement by secular judges, on the doctrine of Holy Baptism, sent many converts over. Archdeacon Manning was one of those who went in 1850. Pusey and Keble, both of whom had been brought up in the old seventeenth-century Prayer Book tradition, remained till they died.

In the next generation the movement passed from Oxford to the slum parishes of London and other great cities. Father Lowder (he was not a professed member of any Community, but he was the kind of priest from whom the title of Father cannot be withheld) gathered a great congregation of devoted people in what was then the rather tough area of Dockland. At St Alban's, Holborn, and St Alban's, Birmingham, and many other places a like work was done. In order to teach their slum people, the priests felt constrained to teach them by the eye as well as the ear. And so they built great churches, with an imposing altar which was manifestly the focus of their worship, and surrounded it with all the dignity that they could compass, lights and music and vestments and ceremonial. In this way the Catholic Revival became in many centres what was commonly called ritualistic. Elsewhere, as in cathedrals for example, it retained a good deal of the austerity of the original Tractarians. Among those who believed in the value of ceremonial there were, and are, two schools, those who followed the strictly English tradition laid down in the Ornaments Rubric of the Book of Common Prayer and those who, either deliberately or unthinkingly, copied the Roman ceremonial.

The third revival was the Christian Social Movement. Always there had been here and there parsons or laymen possessed with the passion for social righteousness, eager to apply their religion to all life. But very many were content to take life, social, economic, and political, as they found it, and to preach and practise the personal Christian virtues. In the nineteenth century a school of Christian Socialists arose. The leader was Frederick Denison Maurice, a man of rare spiritual power, a prophet and a saint. He was not what is now meant by a Socialist. He chose the name as a protest against 'unChristian Socialists and un-social Christians'. He believed intensely that the world really was God's world, that there was a Divine Order which had to be discovered. It was not that we had to improve the life of the world. We only had to perceive what it really and truly was. For this reason he was in some ways unpractical. He did not believe in committees to get things done. That was a human device. He believed only in God. But of a few things he was sure that they were according to the mind of God. The family, the nation, education, and co-operation – these were God-given things, lines along which it was safe to proceed. Thus Maurice was a pioneer in Women's Education (Queen's College, Harley Street), Working Men's Education (the Great Ormond Street College), and in Co-operation. He had able and vigorous lieutenants in J. M. Ludlow, Vansittart Neale, and Tom Hughes, and his chief popularizer was Charles Kingsley.

Some of the later Christian Socialists, e.g. Stewart Headlam, founder of the Guild of St Matthew, and, in more recent times, Conrad Noel, were much more definitely Socialist. The true heirs to Maurice were, however, the leaders of the Christian Social Union (Westcott, Gore,

Holland). The Union was sure about its Christianity, but had no political creed. Some of its members were Socialists, and perhaps a majority were Liberal-Radical. In days when factory inspection was not well developed they compiled 'White Lists' of employers who provided good conditions and paid Trade Union rates of wages. They promoted the sale of leadless glaze pottery, and their monthly journal, *Commonwealth*, edited for many years by Henry Scott Holland, was a tonic for would-be reformers. Holland was always reminding Christian people that, if they believed in the Incarnation, all life was sanctified, and they must care about the Poor Law, about Sweating, and about Drains. One of his most famous Tracts was a reply to those who objected to what they called grandmotherly legislation by the State. Holland retorted, 'But we ourselves are the State.' It was obvious enough, but nobody but Holland would have entitled his tract *Every Man his own Grandmother*.

It is one result of the work of Maurice and his friends, carried on by subsequent generations, that organized Labour in Britain has not been, as often on the Continent, hostile to Christian faith. Among the politicians of recent years who have been supporters of, or influenced by, the C.S.U., were C. F. G. Masterman, George Lansbury, and, it may be added, Mr C. R. Attlee, and, less directly, many others.

Another result of the awakening of the Christian social conscience was the Settlement Movement. Towards the end of last century residents at the Universities, and others whose lives were cast in pleasant places, began to feel acutely that the segregation of classes which had come about, for example, in East London and West London, was a bad thing, and that they, with the cultural and social advantages that they enjoyed, had a responsibility for their neighbours. The father of Settlements was Samuel Barnett. He was Vicar of a slum-parish in Whitechapel, and he paid visits to Oxford and invited Oxford to pay visits to White-chapel and make friends with it. The result of this was

Toynbee Hall. Oxford House in Bethnal Green was founded about the same time, and Oxford College Missions in Poplar, Stratford, and elsewhere. Cambridge went to South London, to Camberwell, Walworth, Rotherhithe, and Battersea, and many of the Public Schools founded Missions of their own. One of the most famous Settlements was 'Oxford and Bermondsey', over which Dr Scott Lidgett presided with great distinction for many years.

It cannot be maintained that even now all Christian people are genuinely conscious of their social duty, but the sense of obligation is increasing. One of the problems is the relation of 'Christian Action' to party politics. If Christian leaders, by speech or otherwise, seek to influence public opinion in such matters as Foreign Affairs, Peace and War, Wage-rates, Housing, they touch party political questions. If they are clergymen, are they to speak of such things in their pulpits? Congregations have been known to complain of 'political sermons', by which they generally mean sermons betraying political opinions which are not their own. The rule for preachers may perhaps be laid down thus: 'Be fair. Do not take advantage of your privileged position. Do not say anything in the pulpit except what the hearers would be unable on purely Christian grounds conscientiously to deny.'

Another element in the situation is that State action is now doing a great deal of what was formerly done by private benevolence. This has its good side. The State has large resources and can give Old Age Pensions or Family Allowances all round, and can provide generously for the treatment of physical and mental ill-health. Thus more is done for those who are in need. On the other hand the prospect of State aid removes incentives for self-discipline, providence, and parental care. What has happened is what has been seen in many walks of life. Voluntary Christian endeavour was the pioneer. It showed the way of service, but it was not strong enough or wealthy enough to meet all the need. The State, having learned the lesson from the pioneers, begins to do the work on a much larger scale, but, as some think, more soullessly. Even now, there is abundant room for voluntary workers, and it has often been noticed that, when there is dull, obscure donkey-work waiting to be done, it is the Christian people, especially the Christian women, who are willing to undertake it.

The fourth revival was the Liberal Movement. The effect of it was to remind Christian people that one of the injunctions of the Ten Commandments was to serve God 'with all thy mind'. It was a much-needed challenge. Ever since the Reformation very many religious people had believed themselves to be committed to the view that the Bible was literally inspired and that every word of it was historically and scientifically true. There was nothing in the Creed or in the authoritative formulas of the Church which required this, but it was in many quarters taken for granted.

The first shock came from Geology. Archbishop Ussher's calculations in the seventeenth century had fixed the date of Creation at 4004 B.C., and the first chapter of Genesis appeared, on the face of it, to say that it had all been accomplished between Sunday and Friday. Geologists now pointed out that the rocks were millions of years old. Some of them, like Hugh Miller, attempted a scientific reconciliation, and there was one earnest believer, himself a scientist of some reputation, who committed himself to the statement that God had created the rocks with the fossils in them. Gradually it came to be recognized that the purpose of Genesis was simply to teach the lesson that God is the Creator. The narrative is in point of fact remarkably scientific. It speaks of stages, sky, sea, earth, vegetation, marine and terrestrial animal life, and finally human life. But we are not intended to take from the story our scientific beliefs. Those are obtained from other quarters.

The next trouble came from Biology. On the strength of Genesis it had been assumed that the species had all been created separately and fully developed. Milton's famous description of the lion emerging from the ground:

> The grassy clods now calved; now half appeared
> The tawny lion, pawing to get free
> His hinder parts – then springs, as broke from bonds,
> And rampant shakes his brinded mane –

had fastened on the popular imagination. Darwin's *Origin of Species* (1859) and *Descent of Man* (1870), although the author in his preface to the former book disclaimed any such purpose, was thought to eliminate the necessity of belief in God. Things, it seemed, had happened by Natural Selection. The best Christian minds found no difficulty in believing in Evolution as the method of Divine Creation, but some whose idea of God had been that of a large Man sitting up in the sky and directing the world by means of miracles (in the earlier centuries), commandments, prophecies, general supervision, and a system of rewards and punishments, were gravely disturbed. As time went on, the religious people gradually saw that their leaders had been right, though there were not a few who exemplified the truth of T. H. Huxley's biting epigram: 'When there is a new thing in science, they first say "It's impossible!" Then they say, "It's against the Bible." Then they say, "We knew it all the time".'

However, worthily or unworthily, the religious people found a way through the apparent difficulty. Meantime many of the scientific men became more arrogant. On the strength of their knowledge of physical science, in which they were experts, they claimed authority in metaphysics or philosophy, in which realm they had no special competence, and pronounced boldly that matter was the origin and explanation of everything. Tyndall's famous Belfast Address (1874) on the Physical Basis of Life represents the high-water mark of this tendency. Since then the natural scientists, led by Poincaré, have become more modest, and have been content to describe, without attempting to explain. It will appear later that, while the biologists are still a little difficult, the physicists have changed their point of view completely and now provide us with descriptions of a universe in which religion, if it is sensible, can thrive abundantly. Theologians must be careful not to be too much uplifted by this, any more than they allowed themselves to be too much cast down by Tyndall's materialism. Theology must not take its conclusions from any other science, however friendly. It must stand on its own legs.

Another quarter in which difficulty arose was that of the Historical Criticism of the Bible. Old-fashioned devout people were terribly disturbed when it was first suggested that the second half of the Book of Isaiah, from Chapter xl onwards, was the work, not of Isaiah, but of an unknown prophet nearly two centuries later, or when it was pointed out that there were two narratives of Creation, the Flood, and much else in the Pentateuch. In fact, the Pentateuch, or rather the Hexateuch, because the Book of Joshua must be included, was resolved into no less than four elements, J, the work of the 'Jehovist', E (Elohist), D (Deuteronomist), and P (the Priestly Writer).

There have been, of course, some extravagances in the critical analysis of the Old Testament. There was a time, for example, not very long ago, when Professor T. K. Cheyne, with the aid of many conjectural emendations of the text, found references to the Musrim of North Arabia and to a mysterious Jerahmeel in a fantastic number of places, but the main results have been thoroughly established. It is also increasingly believed that the reconstruction (for it is no less) of the Old Testament is a great gain to religion. This can be demonstrated, or at least illustrated, in this way. In 1922 Professor Garstang went to Palestine to excavate in the neighbourhood of Jericho. He made certain discoveries, but they did not help him to construct a complete story. He then determined to begin again and examine the archaeology of those parts of the Hexateuch which literary criticism had pronounced to be the oldest. He did so, and it made sense. He produced in *Joshua – Judges* (1931) a scientific and credible story of the crossing of the Jordan by Joshua's army and the fall of Jericho. It had often been supposed (in sermons and elsewhere) that the falling of the walls was simply a picturesque way of saying that the luxury-loving people of Jericho were no match for the hardy, desert-trained invaders, but Garstang found traces of the bulge in the walls which expedited their collapse, and broken remains of pottery of the period, such as might have stood on the shelves of the cupboard of Rahab, the woman who befriended Joshua's spies. It proves two things of considerable importance: (i) that the Old Testament is not a mere conglomeration of incredible legends, and (ii) that it becomes intelligible when it is read critically. Garstang's conclusions have been modified in some respects by later investigators, but the result which emerges is of the same sort.

There was at one time some reason to fear that, with all this criticism, the Old Testament would come to be thought of as not much more than a store-house of antiquarian information about primitive Semitic religion, but there has arisen lately a school of thought which provides a valuable counter-reminder. The whole Bible is thought of as the story of the People of God. In the first volume it is provisional, inchoate, preliminary. Nevertheless Israel is the people to whom God the Creator has made a genuine disclosure of Himself. Whereas Plato reached his conception of God by the way of Discovery, Israel reached it by the way of Revelation. The Bible, even the Old Testament, is the Book of True Religion, the Book which contains the Truth about God and about Man. The criticism is scientific and essential. The gradual evolution, the remains of old paganisms, the inadequacy, sometimes the total absence of national response, are all there. Nevertheless, it is the Bible. There is that in it which could not have come from any other quarter.

Criticism of the New Testament was felt to break more delicate ground. Here, too, there have been extravagances. In the nineteenth century a school of German critics put forward the idea that during the whole New Testament period there was an irreconcilable controversy between Peter and Paul, as severally representing an alleged narrow Palestinian view and a wider, more inclusive view, and that such parts of the New Testament as were authentic and of early date, must be interpreted in the light of this theory. English scholars, especially the famous Cambridge trio, Lightfoot, Westcott, and Hort, as learned as the Germans, but more balanced, had little difficulty in showing that the theological prepossessions of the Tübingen professors had caused them to do violence to the evidence.

D. F. Strauss and E. Renan have been mentioned in an earlier chapter. They were both in different ways guilty of the same error of reaching a verdict first and making selections from the evidence afterwards. German criticism after F. C. Baur of Tübingen receded from the extreme position and allowed earlier dates and a greater degree of authenticity to the New Testament writings, but the picture was still, religiously, rather bleak. In fact, the German Liberal Protestantism which, though it was never adopted wholesale, except here and there, in England, nevertheless had a good deal of influence, was, at its bleakest, the kind of thing described by Browning in his *Christmas Eve and Easter Day*. At its best it was represented by Harnack at the end of the century. He was a Liberal Protestant, but his *What is Christianity?* is full of religious fervour. The story of events in this field since Harnack must be deferred to a later chapter, which will deal with the contemporary situation.

The result of nineteenth-century criticism of the New Testament was to produce unanimity among scholars on a few fundamental points, and some still controverted issues. The Gospel of St Mark is universally acknowledged to be the earliest of the three Synoptic Gospels, though it is generally added that the collection of Sayings (Q) which supplied much of the material for the other two is older still. In St Mark you have true history. In Q you have genuine sayings of the Lord. This does not in the least mean that the remainder is worthless, or even dubious, it only means that in using those two sources you are standing on a rock. St John's Gospel is an interpretation, containing much true history, but it is not easy to distinguish in it between fact and symbolism. Acts is by the author of the Third Gospel, and, though it has an eirenic purpose, it gives a true picture of events. Most of the Pauline Epistles are certainly genuine, though doubt is felt in some quarters about Ephesians and more about Timothy and Titus, at least in their present form. Hebrews is early, and apostolic, but not Pauline. The genuineness of 1 Peter and James is commonly allowed, though there are some hesitations. 2 Peter is certainly not earlier than the second century. The authorship of the Apocalypse is a puzzle. It can hardly be by the author of St John's Gospel, unless it be a generation earlier, and it can hardly be that, because the situation seems more like the reign of Domitian (96) than that of Nero (63).

There is much more that could be said about the New Testament as nineteenth-century criticism leaves it, but this must serve as a summary. The result of the intense fire through which it has passed has been to establish it as a substantially true record of the Ministry of Jesus and the life of the primitive Church.

These four revivals, the Evangelical, the Catholic, the Social, and the Liberal, have all passed over the head of English Christianity in some two hundred years. They have all made their mark everywhere, even where it might least have been expected. Thus Mr Christopher Dawson, a distinguished Roman Catholic historian of thought, has paid this generous tribute to John Wesley, that he 'transformed the whole spiritual climate of eighteenth-century England'.[1] That Roman Catholics do not take their Gospel from John Wesley does not need saying, but inasmuch as Christendom is different because of what Wesley did, the Roman Catholic

1. *Religion and the Modern State*, 123.

Church is different too. The Protestant world was not immediately affected by the Oxford Movement, except in so far as it was in the early years alarmed, and hardened in its Protestantism. Nevertheless, the belief in 'the Catholic Church', the historical sense, and the desire for dignified order in public worship which were behind the Oxford Movement have spread to the Free Churches, and their Sunday service is not now what it was a hundred years ago. Moreover, many of the Free Church leaders have come to exhibit a notable understanding of what is meant by Catholicism. At conferences it occasionally appears that some of the Free Churchmen are more Catholic-minded than some of the Anglicans. Finally, the Social movement and the Liberal movement have made their way everywhere, or very nearly everywhere. It is true that among the Roman Catholics the Liberal movement has encountered certain peculiar difficulties, and the controversy is at the moment in a condition which looks to the outsider rather like stalemate. Perhaps it would be more accurate to say that a *modus vivendi* has been found. And it is also true that in certain regions of both Nonconformity and Anglicanism criticism is still feared and suspected. Nevertheless, it may be said with complete confidence that all four of the movements have made their impression upon all of us. Christendom passed through a number of experiences, and has come out into a wealthier place.

10

Theology To-day

IT was said in the last chapter that Adolf Harnack about
1900 represented the maximum level of German Liberal
Protestantism. Much of his work was done in the fields of
New Testament criticism and the history of dogma. His
popular lectures, given to students of all faculties in the
University of Berlin on 'What is Christianity?' were the
expression of his own religious belief. To him it seemed that
Jesus was the supreme Teacher and Revealer, and that His
message was the Fatherhood of God. To this Alfred Loisy, a
French Abbé, made a reply. He said in L'Évangile et l'Église
that the central thing in the Gospels was the Kingdom of
God. Loisy was in the strict sense a Modernist, that is, a
Catholic who claimed to accept all the results of criticism
and still to be a Catholic. He was suspected of unorthodoxy,
and finally condemned as a heretic. It must be admitted
that he had by that time moved a long way to the left. His
earlier teaching founded a school of Modernists in the
Roman Church, of whom Father George Tyrrell, S.J., was
the most brilliant English-speaking representative. Baron
Friedrich von Hügel, philosopher and saint, was claimed
by some as a Modernist, but, though he criticized freely, he
was very staunch in his theological orthodoxy and in his
adherence to the Church – and he was a layman. Modernism was 'forbidden' by the Papal Encyclical Pascendi in
1907, and since then it has not lifted its head publicly within
the Roman Church. Their theologians, learned, as always,
in philosophical theology, also include many accomplished
Biblical scholars, but their published verdicts do not conflict
with the requirements of ecclesiastical authority. The
ground of the official disapproval of Modernism was that it

was alleged to consider religious truth a matter of opinion, whereas in fact it was a matter of Revelation. Revelation consisted for the most part of the original deposit, but also of the inspired teaching of the Church in later centuries.

Another quite different sort of suggestion was launched on Christendom from another quarter. At about the same time it began to be said by some that Paul was the real creator of Christianity, that he succeeded in transforming an original, simple 'faith of Jesus', a religion of 'Love God and love your neighbour', into a regular Greek mystery-religion complete with Redeemer-God and Sacraments. The answer to it was first that, although St Paul very sensibly used from time to time terminology which would be intelligible to his Greek converts from heathenism, he was both too ineradicably Jewish, and also too closely watched, to have brought about anything like the transformation alleged. And in the second place the supposed simple 'religion of Jesus' turns out on examination never to have existed at all.

At about the same time there came what really was rather a thunderbolt. It had, of course, always been known that towards the end of all three Synoptic Gospels there occurred a long eschatological discourse, which seemed partly to be about the Fall of Jerusalem and partly about the end of the world. There were also passages in the Epistles which seemed to expect a speedy return of the Lord in glory to judge the world. These had been rather by-passed, as neither very interesting nor very important. Albert Schweitzer suddenly affirmed that all this, and much more in the New Testament, which he claimed as akin to this, was of the essence of primitive Christianity. Christianity was apocalyptic, much as the second half of the Book of Daniel is apocalyptic. The parables looked forward to a coming Judgement, the Lord's Prayer was governed by the clause 'Thy Kingdom come'. Even the ethical teaching was provisional, an *interim Ethik*, a few rules issued to cover the period till 'the Day' should come. Jesus Himself continually expected that the Heavenly Father would miraculously intervene on His behalf and suddenly bring in the New World, and, when nothing happened, He died on the Cross, broken-hearted.

This was very startling. It was above all a blow to the old Liberalism, the interpretation of Christianity as a method for the peaceful penetration of society by improved ethical ideas, or, in Matthew Arnold's words, 'morality touched by emotion'.

The Schweitzer position was found to be an exaggeration. There was indeed that element in early Christianity, more integral than had been supposed, but it was not the whole story. The Kingdom in the Gospels is spoken of sometimes as future, but sometimes also as present. For, where the King is, there is the Kingdom. Schweitzer himself later receded from his extreme view. He allowed that there was in St Paul's religion a mystical quality which was permanent and independent of any particular eschatological expectation. He still called it eschatological mysticism, but that was because he was so wedded to the term. And Schweitzer himself remained a Christian missionary in Africa, a fact which had seemed to some rather hard to reconcile with the surface implications of his original book, but proved that he was not putting forward his theory as an attack on Christianity, or as a substitute for it, but as a clue to its real meaning.

The main body of Christian theologians used Schweitzer as they have used many a new and revolutionary suggestion. They rejected its extravagances, and sucked from it, as the Psalmist says, no small advantage. So learned a scholar and so sober a theologian as Dr Headlam, then Bishop of Gloucester, said 'Apocalyptic is Religion'. There is, of course, in Christianity an evolutionary element, but there is also a catastrophic or revolutionary element. The Christian life does not consist simply in listening to the good advice which Jesus of Nazareth gives. It is more like a sort of perpetual season of Advent. It was at least a remarkable coincidence, as was pointed out by Professor Burkitt of

Cambridge, one of Schweitzer's most brilliant English interpreters, that the rediscovery of apocalyptic became generally known at the time of a world war. It was made apparent that Christianity was a religion for a day of crisis, and that the character which would survive was that which feared not to ride upon the very wings of storm itself.

Another school of thought had for a time a considerable influence among scholars, though it has not become well known at the popular level. A method called *Form-Geschichte* or Form-Criticism was applied to the interpretation of the New Testament. The theory was that the Sermon was the beginning of everything. The kind of sermon that Peter delivered on his missionary journeys was the origin of the Gospels. Traditional sayings of Jesus gradually acquired a narrative framework. Thus it was thought possible in St Mark's Gospel to distinguish a Mark I, a Mark II, and a Mark III, different stages through which the material passed in the circumstances of missionary preaching and teaching. The method in the hands of many of its German representatives reduced the genuinely historical element in the Gospels to very small dimensions, but their results have not commanded general assent. The method remains one and one only of the tools with which to handle an intricate problem or series of problems.

The obvious comments are that it is all very subjective, and also presupposes that there was no original and continuous Church-memory. 'If the Form Critics are right', says Professor Vincent Taylor, 'the disciples must have been translated to Heaven immediately after the Resurrection'. Nevertheless, as he readily allows, the method is one that can be used with good results.

Two other things remain to be mentioned in this field. In Germany after the first War there arose a prophet, Karl Barth. He did much to arrest the decay of post-war German morale, and to turn many of the would-be suicides to a stronger purpose and a better hope. He revived the old Augustinian doctrine of the Sovereignty of God. God was all. Man was nothing. God judges. God saves. God never explains. Man's part is to bend his head humbly, and take, unquestioningly, what God shall send. It was a grim message, but full of power, and it has had an immense influence not only in Germany but all over the non-Catholic parts of European Christendom. The present writer, attending a seminar in Geneva in 1937, expounded an ordinary Anglican view of what might be called 'co-operation with God'. Some of the continentals, French, Dutch, and Scandinavian, were startled, even shocked. 'But what becomes', they said, 'of the Divine Sovereignty?'

Barth has had many disciples in England, some very whole-hearted, others with reservations. A Cambridge scholar, Sir Edwyn Hoskyns, blazed a trail which satisfied some of the instincts which were being met elsewhere by Barth. Hoskyns was not himself a Barthian. He at first knew little of him, though he later translated Barth's great commentary on the Epistle to the Romans, but he was a parallel force. With Noel Davey, he wrote *The Riddle of the New Testament*. It was, among other things, one more blow to the old Liberalism. But that was only a result. The book was, in itself, a critical examination of the Gospels. It took them to pieces in the usual way and it found in every strand, the Markan and the non-Markan material, the parables, the miracles, the isolated sayings, not imported into the material by any author or editor, but inherent in the material itself, the same picture. And the picture was not in the least the old humanitarian picture, beloved of nineteenth-century Liberalism, but a picture of a Figure at every point Messianic, prophecy-fulfilling, apocalyptic, superhuman, divine. There were, as is natural, exaggerations in the book. Not all the Old Testament words used in the Gospels were deliberate, calculated quotations. Yet in the main it was a convincing picture. The Jesus of the old, mild Liberalism would not have made upon the world for nineteen centuries the deep and regenerating impact which has in fact been made.

It is perhaps not too much to say that Hoskyns and Davey provided the scholarly formulation for an impression recorded as long ago as 1907 by G. K. Chesterton:

> Instead of looking at books and pictures about the New Testament, I looked at the New Testament. There I found an account, not in the least of a person with his hair parted in the middle or with his hands clasped in appeal but of an extraordinary being with lips of thunder and acts of lurid decision, flinging down tables, casting out devils, passing with the wild secrecy of the wind from mountain isolation to a sort of dreadful demogogy; a King who often acted like an angry god – and always like a god.[1]

Hoskyns and Davey did this, not as theologians, still less as advocates with any kind of axe to grind, but as critical historians, anxious to explore the truth. Their results, however, gave much support to a conviction which has been growing everywhere during the last generation, that the New Testament is a thoroughly Semitic book, and that the Christian religion will never be understood unless the Christian Scriptures are seen to be continuous with those of the earlier Revelation. This conception and use of the Scriptures is commonly spoken of as Biblical Theology, and it is because both Anglicans and Free Churchmen in England are students of Biblical Theology that the Agreed Syllabuses, prepared by Joint Committees and used in Provided Schools, are so much stronger, religiously and theologically, than they could possibly have been thirty years ago.

We step into a quite different region of ideas when we face the question of the relation of religion and Physical Science. In the last century the controversy seemed very acute, and was in fact considerable. This was in part because religion took some time to adjust itself to the new knowledge, and in part because some of the scientific men staked claims in a region where they had no special competence, and in the name of Natural Science commended Materialist Philosophy. What its exponents call the New Physics has

1. *Orthodoxy*, 269.

altered all that. Science of all kinds has become more modest, more willing to admit that its task is to measure and to describe rather than to explain. Einstein has made it clear that our measurements, true enough within the frame of earthly life, are not absolute. They are 'true', but not 'really true'. Moreover, physical researches have turned the atom from the tiny billiard-ball which it was once supposed to be, into a unit of force, a pointer reading in a schedule. The old Determinism is no longer preached, and the world is delivered from the iron mould in which in the last century it was imprisoned. Prediction, in the old confident way, is no longer possible. Finally, the universe, as described by the science of physics, is so abstract, so wholly a series of formulas, that it is quite obviously not the real world in which life is lived. Scientific men who are practising Christians are shy of attempting to indicate the bearing of their new interpretation of nature on such things as miracle or 'direct' answer to prayer, but the obvious moral is that there are more things in heaven and earth than were dreamt of in the old philosophy of science. The world, as described by scientific men, cries aloud for some kind of explanation by philosophers or theologians.

It cannot, of course, be denied that there are some scientific men who are contemptuous of Christian theology, and some who to their ignorance of it add indifference. And there are some who, being religious men, keep their religion in a separate compartment, who say: 'My science gives me nothing but materialism (or mechanism), but I cross the corridor into the chapel, or I kneel down in my bedroom, and there my religious experience is valid.' It is a brave and interesting attempt to live in two worlds, but it would seem that a more monistic philosophy, that is, referring all phenomena to a single category, however difficult it may be to compass, is more worth attempting. 'Science valid, religion valid' may meet the personal needs of one pilgrim, but the combination, if it can be attained, of religious science and scientific religion makes a better map for general use.

The relation of Christianity with the philosophers is more complicated and more difficult. Idealism, the old ally of Theism, is considered in many quarters to have been dethroned, and it has been replaced by various kinds of Realism. Some of it, like Bergson's Creative Evolution or Whitehead's definition of God as 'the Principle of Concretion', in which he says that it is impossible not to believe, or Lloyd Morgan's doctrine of Emergent Evolution, which begins, he says, with Naturalism and leads to 'the open door of the Cathedral of Christianity', has been found useful by Christian thinkers. Alexander's doctrine of the God who is only gradually emerging into existence is naturally less satisfying. Other writers put forward a doctrine of God which is expressed in religious language, but on examination turns out to be no more than a personification of man's best ideas. And there are some who approach as near to Atheism as it is possible to go. The Logical Positivists and the Existentialists (some of the latter are, like Kierkegaard, Christian Existentialists) agree in questioning the validity of metaphysics, but many others are of the opinion that Plato and Aristotle and the old classical tradition of philosophy cannot easily be dethroned. There is also an important school of Neo-Scholastics, who present the thought of Thomas Aquinas in an attractive modern dress.

A word to conjure with in recent years has been Psychology. It is an intensely interesting subject, because it classifies and rationalizes many of the things about which everybody knows, and everybody wonders, dreams, old instincts which recur, likes and dislikes, family troubles, shyness, assertiveness, the way in which one thing brings up another, and so forth. The plain man is always pleased to have an experience like that of M. Jourdain, when he found that all his life he had been speaking prose. There are Christian psychologists and anti-Christian psychologists, but in neither case is it their psychology which really leads them to their theological or non-theological belief. Psychology is not metaphysical. It can compare a man's belief in God with a child's reliance on a parent, it can describe prayer as a projection of the self, but it cannot, out of its own resources, determine that the man's belief is an illusion or that the projection does not find an end. That is the province of other lines of study. But new sciences are always rather over-ambitious.

The popularity of psychology, and the not uncommon impression that Freud has reduced religion to a complex or to wishful thinking or infantilism, has led to a re-examination by Christian thinkers of the argument from religious experience. Some are content to say, 'Follow the saints, the great mystics, who have trodden the high places. They have been there. They know.' Others, more wisely, interpret religious experience in a large way, as meaning the entire experience of religious people. Among the relevant facts to be considered are the general sense that such people have that their religion helps them to live better lives than they could without it, their sense that when they pray or worship there is Someone at the other end, the way in which such people work and play and say grace over their meat, and perhaps above all, the way in which such people behave when their consciences tell them that they have done something wrong. All this is a very large volume of human experience, in Christianity and in other religions. It may conceivably be an illusion, but, if it is, it is a very large and very old one, and it needs much courage, not to say impudence, to pronounce out of hand that it is wholly invalid.

The argument from experience has been reinforced by Professor Rudolf Otto, with his new category of the numinous. There can be, he says, in persons, places, and things a quality to which he gives that name: a saint, a church, a sacrament, a lonely place like Dartmoor at sunset or sunrise, is numinous. The word, in his definition, has a twofold meaning. The numinous attracts and at the same time alarms. It is a *mysterium* at once *fascinosum* and *tremendum*. This was more simply put by John Keble in his hymn for Holy Communion:

> It is my Maker! – Dare I stay?
> My Saviour – Dare I turn away?

Anything like a thorough exploration of this category would take us very far. It has been much used by religious persons as a means of analysing their experience, but it would certainly be a mistake to rest the whole case for Christianity on a foundation so mystical and hard to verify. Impressions of numinousness are not common property, and are hard, if not impossible, to communicate. Some other approach to reality is essential, not of necessity instead of this, but side by side with it. And with the other approach the intellect and also the will must be concerned. Bishop Gore was accustomed to say that *Agapé*, the New Testament word for the highest kind of love, the love of God, or man's love for God, was not a thing of the emotions at all. It was a matter of the will, and it must have reason to support it. Perhaps it might be said that there are three worlds, those of history, reason, and spiritual experience, in which the Christian religion, or any religion, may fairly be required to make good. If the events on which it rests never happened, if its case be contrary to reason, if it fails altogether in the region where *cor ad cor loquitur*, then it must go.

Thus, while there is no ground for believing that everybody in the world will in this life eventually be converted and convinced, the battle is still proceeding upon all three fronts. There are those who would rewrite our history, who question our reasonings, who discount our experience, but the faith which once sustained an old Hebrew writer still sustains the Christian Church. 'The plowers plowed upon my back: and made long furrows. Yea, many a time have they vexed me from my youth up: but they have not prevailed against me.' Or, to use a rather more definitely hostile metaphor from Genesis, 'The archers have sorely grieved him, and shot at him, and hated him: but his bow abode on strength, and the arms of his hands were made strong by the hands of the mighty God of Jacob.' Those who arrogate to themselves the title of Rationalists often claim to have pulverized Christianity, but it is a fair retort, if it be not deemed irreverent, to use our Lord's own words, that a heap of dust 'hath not flesh and bones, as ye see me have.'

I I

Expansion and Unity

THE word commonly used to express the developments of
Christendom in lands which have hitherto been non-
Christian has had hard treatment. Some of those who have
been most complacent about the magnitude of the area
over which the English language is spoken, or the Empire
over which the British flag waves, or until lately, since a
different policy has been adopted, most eager that political
dominion should be enlarged, have been most apt to sneer
or snort when there is talk of missions. And others are
either ignorant of what is happening or strangely blind to
the significance of the fact that Asia and Africa are gradually becoming Christian.

The criticism arises partly from a lightly-reached
impression that the African or other non-Christian is best
left with his own religion, or from some isolated or perhaps
even second-hand reminiscence of a 'Mission-trained'
servant, perhaps a boy who had picked up a smattering at
a Mission School and had then run away and drifted into
the labour market, 'English-speaking', 'Mission-trained'.
The fact that he is a thief and a liar is put down to the
Mission School! As if it could seriously be believed that
Christ had made him worse!

The answer to the first criticism is very simple. In the
first place is Animism or Obi true? And in the second
place *laisser-faire* is impossible. European and American
habits and ways of life – it would be a misuse of terms to
say that the effect of them everywhere could be called
civilization – are spreading, and old faiths are crumbling.
The alternatives are Christianity or nothing. And the
nothing would really be a minus quantity, because dis-

illusionment in religion carries a man beyond zero into debt.

The best answer to the second criticism is 'Go, and see'. Go, like Charles Darwin, to Tierra del Fuego, where he saw what made him a subscriber to the Mission. Or go, like the airman who during the war made a forced landing on a remote Pacific island, and wrote home, 'Dear Mum, Thanks to Missions, I was feasted and not feasted upon, when I came down on this island.' Or, if you want to know what African Christianity can be, read Paton's *Cry, the Beloved Country*. Or consider the fact that Zanzibar Cathedral is built on the site of the old slave-market, and that whereas in 1858 David Livingstone said to the University in the Senate House at Cambridge, 'Gentlemen, I leave it to you', there are now, in what is called the Universities' Mission to Central Africa, four bishops, many of the most devoted, selfless priests, sisters, and laymen in the world, and many thousands of eager African Christian worshippers, who, without being Europeanized, have become disciples of the Master. Consider the deep penetration of educated India and Pakistan by Christian ideas which has been brought about by the University Missions at Calcutta, Delhi, and Cawnpore. Have you ever heard of Tyndale-Biscoe in Kashmir? of Johnson in Nyasaland? of Studd in China? Do you know what George Selwyn did for white men and dark men in New Zealand, including the sad period of the Maori wars? Ask what Field Marshal Smuts thought of the S.P.G. Industrial Missions in South Africa? Or ask the Colonial Office why they had no hesitation in deciding that the College of Achimota must be a Christian college?

Perhaps this most stirring chapter in the Anglican missionary history of the last few generations is that of Uganda. In November 1875 H. M. Stanley, the explorer, wrote from the Court of Mtesa, King of Uganda, to the *Daily Telegraph*, that Christian teachers would be welcomed in that part of Africa. An anonymous donor offered £5,000 to the Church Missionary Society if they would at once seize the opportunity. They did. It was a dangerous experiment. Uganda was an unknown country, separated from the coast by a thousand miles of forest. Little was known about the treatment of African tropical diseases. Out of the eight men, of whom seven were laymen, who sailed in April 1876, two died almost immediately, two were sent home sick, and two were murdered. But one of the remainder was Alexander Mackay, an engineer, and a man of heroic spiritual fibre. He set up his forge, taught young Baganda men his craft and his faith, and learned languages. The first four baptisms were in 1881, and by 1883 there were eighty more.

In a few years there was a new king, Mwanga, a cruel tyrant. He tortured and killed hundreds of his Christian subjects. A bishop, James Hannington, had been consecrated for Eastern Equatorial Africa. Mwanga arrested him on the way out and after eight days of imprisonment, racked with fever and starvation, he was murdered. His diary exists, and his last words were, 'Tell Mwanga that I have purchased the road to Uganda with my life.'

Mwanga went on killing Christians, who showed marvellous fortitude. The second bishop, Parker, died of fever on his way to Uganda. Mackay went on, constantly threatened, but the threats stopped short of death. He printed St Matthew's Gospel and the Baptismal Service in the Baganda language. When someone at home suggested that the Mission should be abandoned, he wrote:

If you tell me in earnest that such a suggestion has been made I only answer NEVER.

After fourteen years in Africa without leave, he wrote:

What is this you write – 'Come home?' Surely now, in our terrible dearth of workers it is not the time for anyone to desert his post.

A month after writing this, he died of fever.

After this things became easier. The blood of the martyrs is always the seed of the Church. The third bishop, Tucker, in his second year saw 5,000 Africans at the Christmas Day services. Soon forty chiefs set all their slaves free. Pilkington, a linguistic genius, translated the whole of the New Testament and eventually the whole Bible. Schools sprang up everywhere. A brick Cathedral was built. Women missionaries were brought in. The villages were evangelized, the Baganda people themselves being the chief missionaries. On 26 October 1947, the first African Anglican Bishop was consecrated, in the presence of more than a hundred of the clergy, black and white, and 3,000 representatives of the 200,000 Christians of the diocese. It had been a very tough fight. It was by no means ended in 1947, but another very splendid chapter had been added to the 'Acts of the Apostles'. Africa had brought some of its glory into the City of God. The sons of Simon of Cyrene had come into their inheritance.

In the story of Free Church Missions there is no figure more splendid than that of William Carey, the Baptist shoemaker. He was that, and Sydney Smith, Canon of St Paul's, to his shame, sneered at him as 'a sanctified cobbler', but he made himself, even before he laid the foundations of Christianity in India, much more than a shoemaker. Born in 1761, and apprenticed to his trade, he read books of geography and travel, and his mind began to be filled with thoughts of the spiritual plight of heathendom. He taught himself enough to become a schoolmaster, and eventually a minister. He studied languages, Greek, Latin, Hebrew, Italian, French, and Dutch, but all the time his main preoccupation was the conviction that the Lord's command to make disciples of all nations was as binding now as it had been in the beginning. His fellow-Baptists were not at that time very missionary-hearted. Many of them were Calvinists, and disposed to say to the young enthusiast, 'When the Lord is pleased to convert the heathen, He will do it without the help of you or me.' He wrote a book, *An Enquiry into the Obligation of Christians to use Means for the Conversion of the Heathen*. This, and a stirring sermon delivered by him at a Congress at Nottingham in 1792, won them over and led to the foundation of a Baptist Missionary Society. Two men, John Thomas and Carey himself, volunteered to go to India.

It was not easy even to get there. The East India Company's ships would not take missionaries, but they sailed from Dover in June 1793, in a Dutch vessel. Forbidden to labour on British-controlled soil, they began under the Dutch flag at Serampore. There was not much money coming from England, and Carey supported himself first as a planter, and later as a lecturer in a Government College in Bengali and Sanskrit. He earned in fact a great deal, and contributed very large sums to the Society. He built a college at Serampore, and inaugurated the work of translating the Bible and training Indian teachers. Among the other pioneers was John Chamberlain, who had been a plough-boy in Northamptonshire. When someone criticized the missionaries as 'low-born and low-bred mechanics', Andrew Fuller replied, 'These low-born and low-bred mechanics have translated the whole Bible into Bengali and have by this time printed it. They are printing the New Testament in the Sanskrit, Orissa, Mahratta, Hindustani.'

Of these men one was originally a shoemaker, another a printer at Hull, and a third the master of a charity school at Bristol. In 1940, 147 years after Carey's arrival in India, the Baptist community alone had in India 175 European missionaries, 806 Indian workers, 496 churches, 27,331 communicant members, and there were in that year 1,579 baptisms. It warrants a quotation from the Acts of the Apostles: 'So mightily grew the word of God and prevailed.'

Among Roman Catholics there are thousands of devoted missionaries to-day. It is said that there is in France an institution for the training of missionary priests which possesses among its treasures a chalice once used in China by a priest who in some period of violent upheaval was torn in pieces by bandits. Every student, after being ordained priest for service abroad, says Mass in the College Chapel, using this chalice. Not a few of them have since then been martyrs themselves. Yet in some respects the great period was that of the Counter-Reformation in the sixteenth and seventeenth centuries. And this was the more remarkable because at that time the Reformed or Reforming Churches, preoccupied with their own internal reorganization, were doing almost no missionary work. One of the great names is that of Bartolome de las Casas (1474–1566). He was of a noble and wealthy family, and he had no thought at first of becoming either a missionary or a Dominican Friar. He went to the West Indies to manage his father's estates, and there he had Indian slaves, like any other Spaniard. What was remarkable was that he treated them kindly. In 1510 he was, rather surprisingly, ordained priest, without, as it would seem, very much sense of vocation. Very soon he experienced a conversion. He had witnessed in Cuba some indescribable cruelties, and he returned to Spain in order to prosecute a crusade against the indiscriminate exploitation of the Indian people. It was unpopular in many quarters and at times he went in danger of his life. There is a tradition that it was he who introduced African slavery into the New World. The fact is that there were African slaves in America as early as 1500. In 1517 las Casas incautiously agreed to the request of some colonists that the King of Spain be asked to consent to the importation of more Africans to replace those whom he was setting free. He soon repented even of this, but his memory still labours under an unjust accusation. A modern student of the period, the Rev. David Jenks, not himself a Roman Catholic, has written:

In the whole history of foreign missions there is possibly not another man who more richly deserves the name of the Apostle of the Indians than this Spaniard. For half a long life he fought the battle of land appropriation three centuries before English missionaries began to be distressed about it. He pleaded before kings, cardinals, and royal councils; he was habitually opposed by the more self-interested of the clergy; and yet this man, beloved only by the Indians, and who might have enjoyed the pleasant society of Seville and of the court, or have found his delight in those intellectual pursuits for which he was well equipped, is to-day scarcely ever mentioned other than by a brief reference to him as the man who introduced slavery into America.

He lived to the age of ninety-two. He became a Dominican, and eventually a Bishop. He was not always discreet, but he was always a fighter on the side of the oppressed. He left his literary remains to a College in Spain, and wrote in his will: 'Let them be placed in the College library *ad perpetuam rei memoriam*; for should God decree the destruction of Spain, it may be seen that it is because of our destruction of the Indies, and His justice may be made.'

These fragments of missionary history, from three phases of Christianity and from different periods, suggest that it is time that the ordinary ignorant English critic of overseas missions revised his opinions in the light of facts. The old picture of the missionary as a gentleman in a long coat, sitting under a palm-tree, and distributing copies of the Scriptures to the assembled natives, has long ceased to bear any resemblance to the truth. The missionary to-day may be a priest, or a sister, or a doctor, or a nurse, or a school-master, or an engineer, or a printer, or a linguistic expert who compiles the grammar and dictionary of a hitherto un-written vernacular. In any of these callings he may find himself at times compelled to act as if he were a statesman, a psychologist, a judge, a geographer, a father of the dis-tressed. When Bishop Frank Weston of Zanzibar, having received the temporary rank of Major in the First World War, organized and commanded a Carrier Corps of some 2,000 men, his discipline and his efficiency were such that a mining magnate from the Rand said to him: 'I don't know who you are, sir, but if you want a job after this war, come to me and we shan't quarrel about terms.' The palm-tree of the picture has turned into a church, built of local materials in the indigenous style, in which the language of the country and a Christian version of the music to which the people are accustomed is heard every day, or it is a school, hospital, or workshop. The Bible Society has translated the Bible or parts of it into 808 languages, and S.P.C.K. has issued or sponsored 140 translations of the Prayer Book or parts of it.

What is the motive behind all this? Ultimately, the motive is what the old Duke of Wellington used to call 'Our marching orders, gentlemen', the injunction, 'Go ye into all the world, and make disciples of all nations.' The content of this injunction is in the first instance quite simple. It is the desire that there shall be more and more nations, and consequently more and more persons, who are disciples of Christ. But there is more in it than that. It is not merely arithmetic, counting heads. In a democratic system, the will of the majority prevails. But believers in democracy feel that there is what Lord Bryce once called 'a mystical will' of the people, which does not always express itself correctly in the hurry and turmoil of an election, but emerges over a large area and in the long run. The best method of rehousing the population of a country after a war may be one of the issues at an election, but it is plainly the desire of the human race that there should be families and homes. In the same way, in religion, a numerous Church is likely to be powerful and to have influence in the world, but the heraldry of Christendom is hearts, and not, after the manner of arithmetic, heads. And this means more than the obvious truism that the converts ought to be good and genuine converts. The words of A. C. Ainger's hymn:

> God is working his purpose out, as year succeeds to year,
> God is working his purpose out, and the time is drawing near.
> Nearer and nearer draws the time, the time that shall surely be,
> When the earth shall be filled with the glory of God as the waters
> cover the sea.

are not satisfied by the mere receiving of a good report about the state of the converts. The glory of God is a much larger thing than that.

What it means can be discovered by an examination of St Paul's doctrine of the Body of Christ. St Paul had a missionary strategy. He moved from one large centre of population and culture to another, and his purpose was to build up the Body of Christ, with all the various sorts of human material that were available. It is expressed in the following words:

> For the perfecting of the saints, for the work of the ministry, for the edifying of the body of Christ: Till we all come in the unity of the faith, and of the knowledge of the Son of God, unto a perfect man, unto the measure of the stature of the fulness of Christ.
>
> (Eph. iv, 12, 13.)

and, even more incisively (if the English reader, in spite of both the Authorized and Revised Version, will take my word for it that the Greek word *pleroumenou* really has a passive meaning) in 'The Church, the fulness of him who is (thereby) all in all fulfilled' (Eph. i, 23). Compare with these some words from almost the last chapter of the New Testament, a picture of the City of God, into which first the kings of the earth, and then, better still, the nations of the earth, are to bring their glory.

The meaning is that each nation has something to contribute to the fulness of the Body. It is quite apparent that the English have something of their own, because the story of the English Church has been, and English Christianity continuously is, different from that in other countries. There has also been an Italian, a French, a German, and a Russian Christianity. Looking further ahead, Westcott was accustomed to say that we shall not understand the Gospel of St John until there grows up a large-scale Indian Christianity. The Chinese, if they still have their family affection and their devotion to the memory of ancestors, have something to teach Western Christendom in the appreciation of the Christian doctrine of the Communion of Saints. The patriotism of the Japanese, turned in a new direction, would illuminate fresh possibilities of devotion to a truly Divine Emperor. In like manner, the African Negro, the Maori, the Melanesian, have a glory to bring in. Some of it has already been brought in, but until all the potentialities which have been mentioned, and far more than that, have been realized in conversion, the Body of Christ will not have been built up, the fulness will not have come true. Once again observe the amazing audacity of the Pauline passive, 'Christ fulfilled'. The Lord Christ will wait, it seems, till His Body has its full complement of members. The Venerable Bede, when he rose from his studies to take his part with the brothers at the hour of Terce or Sext or None, used to say, 'If I am not there, the angels will ask, Where is Bede?' Are there not voices even now which ask, as the Church of Christ grows, 'But where is China, or Persia, or Basutoland?' 'Ring in the Christ that is to be.'

This then is the real motive for missionary work, and the real meaning of 'Go ye into all the world, and make disciples of all nations.' It is not only that the nations may have Christ. It is that Christ may have the nations.

English people who live in England, whose reading is limited to secular books and secular newspapers, have no conception of the speed with which Christendom is growing in the East, or of the solidity and importance of what has come into existence. The younger Churches, as they like to call themselves, are developing an outlook, a policy, and, it may be added, an impatience with European slowness which is full of encouragement.

What is the chief obstacle to such work? We may dismiss for the present purpose such causes as the limited number of missionaries, or the comparatively small amount of money available, because that only means that less work can be done. It is a very serious handicap, because there are fields only waiting to be harvested, but it does not impair the quality or value of what is done. The thing that does that is the great and outstanding blemish upon Christendom, its disunited state.

The scandal is grosser overseas than at home. Our divisions have a long history, and at home we have become accustomed to them. But why, it may well be asked, must we carry our difficulties, which arose out of the accidents of

English or European history, to virgin soil? Up to a point it may be said that in fact we do not. There is a widely-used principle, the Comity of Missions, by which Roman Catholic, Anglican, and non-episcopal missionaries agree to occupy different parts of a country. But this is only a local palliative. The Indian or the African Christian knows very well that on the other side of the hills is another different kind of Christian Mission, with which he is not in full communion. This often makes him very impatient. The creation of the United South India Church, an experiment which some at home are watching with hope and some with apprehension, is the result of a felt need for unifying action. Other like experiments are being planned elsewhere. The scandal of disunion is much more than an obstacle to missionary work. It is the chief reproach of Christendom. A good deal has been done in recent years towards its ultimate removal, but breaches which have endured for four hundred years, or, in one great case, for more than twice as long as that, will not be quickly healed.

No sensible person supposes that all Christians will take, or should take, precisely the same view of what Christianity is. Christianity is a big thing, and not only can it not be expected that any one set of disciples will comprehend the whole of it, but it is even salutary that different groups should emphasize different aspects. There are at least four types of Christian discipleship, the Eastern Orthodox, the Roman Catholic, the Anglican, the non-episcopal Protestant. To these perhaps should be added the Friends, a small but well-marked and valuable element in Christendom. It is not here suggested that one is as good as another, or that it does not matter to which type a man belongs, but at least the variety ensures a broad-based attempt to do justice to what St Paul calls the unsearchable riches of Christ.

The trouble is not that we take different views. So far as that goes, it is probable that there are many individuals in every separated part who have more in common with the characteristic beliefs of some other part than with some of those commonly held in their own community: and the trouble is not that united action is impossible. The easy taunt of the man in the street, 'Why can't they get together?' is out of date. They do get together. There is plenty of common action. Even the Roman Catholics, who have, on principle, the largest measure of scruple about anything which might seem to endanger or qualify their own definition of 'The Church', have found it possible in recent years, under the title of 'The Sword of the Spirit', to combine with non-Roman Christians for some good purposes. And in England, and doubtless elsewhere, there is a great deal of co-operation between Anglicans and Free Churchmen.

The trouble is much deeper than that. There is no inter-communion. Except among non-episcopal Protestants, who are as a rule ready to welcome any Christian brother to their Sacrament, the altars are fenced. Free Churchmen are not in the ordinary way invited to the altar of the Parish Church, and in no circumstances are Free Church Ministers invited to celebrate Holy Communion in the Parish Church. Anglicans are not invited to the altars of the Roman Church and Orthodox and Romans are not in communion with one another. There is not at present inter-communion between Orthodox and Anglican, but they are on very friendly terms with one another, and inter-communion is, so to speak, on the way. When the Orthodox theologians are satisfied that Anglican Orders are free from irregularity, a point on which some of them have already reached affirmative conclusions, and others are still undecided, it will no doubt come.

All this seems to the outsider very intolerant, but there is a reason for it. The nerve-system of the Church is the Ministry, and the traditional theory of the Ministry is that Holy Orders are conferred by the laying-on of episcopal hands. Those who adhere to this theory are bound to consider that there is something lacking in the ministerial standing of those who have been admitted to their ministry in some other way, and those who further maintain that the only true Bishops are those of their own communion are bound to consider that clergymen otherwise admitted to their ministry are really laymen.

There is here what looks like a deadlock, but from a deadlock which is felt by the great majority of thoughtful Christian leaders to be intolerable some way out will eventually be found.

East and West fell apart as long ago as 1054. Even then Rome and Constantinople had long been drifting asunder, and for centuries after that they knew very little about one another. It is hardly for a non-Roman Western to suggest what could be done to heal this oldest and greatest of all the breaches in Christian unity, but many of us hope that two great Churches, which trace back their ancestry to primitive Rome and primitive Jerusalem, will not permanently be estranged. The difficulty from the Western side is that the Orthodox do not admit that it is essential to be in communion with the Pope, and from the Eastern side that the Westerns have added to the Faith. But if a *modus vivendi* could be established, it might ripen into some kind of organic union. There is no prospect whatever of uniformity, but that, as has been said, is not to be expected or desired.

Anglican difficulties on the Romeward side are much the same as those of the Orthodox. There are some Anglicans who hate and fear Popery as an evil thing, but most of them admire the ancient and splendid structure, and if certain conditions could somehow be modified and certain Anglican traditions and liberties somehow preserved, would have little difficulty in allowing a primacy to the Bishop of Rome as the traditional head of the Western Church. Sensible Anglicans are aware of the danger of insularity and provincialism in their religion, but at the same time they are extremely unlikely to throw away or to deny their own inheritance, which indeed dates in very many things from long before the Reformation. A correspondence in *The Times* in November 1949 revealed the existence in some of the Roman Catholic writers of a genuine desire at least for better feeling and a larger degree of co-operation.

F 2

The relations of Anglicans and non-episcopalians are more promising, not because Anglicans are actually nearer to non-episcopalians than they are to Roman or Orthodox, but because the leaders of both sides are making determined efforts to heal the breach. It is now generally agreed that the history of episcopacy in Christendom is such that the Church of the future will be episcopal. This does not involve what is commonly called prelacy, and an episcopal Church may well have in it Presbyterian and Congregationalist elements. The problem is how to pass on episcopacy to the non-episcopal Churches in such a way that they will not feel that they are repudiating their own past history or denying their own spiritual experience.

What is called the 'Oecumenical' idea, the conception of the Christian Church as *Una Sancta*, in spite of physical divisions, has made great strides in recent years. The Lausanne Conference in 1927 and others since have revealed not only a great desire for organic unity, but the actual existence of a very deep and strong unity in faith and purpose. Orthodox, Anglicans, and non-episcopalians have all taken part in these and Roman Catholics, unable themselves to take part in them, have watched them with deep and increasing interest. Among the great names in this connexion are Bishop Brent of U.S.A., Archbishop Söderblom of Uppsala and Archbishop William Temple of Canterbury.

Ever since the Lambeth Conference in 1920 the idea has been, except in one quarter, not the absorption of one Church into another, or of all into one, but the great Church of the future. It is admitted, though again not everywhere, that no Church is truly Catholic, because no Church, ministering its means of grace, has with it and behind it a united Christendom. The Church of the future will contain whatever any considerable body of Christian people have ever seriously stood for. It may have its groups, its guilds, its differences of tradition and emphasis. There might be in England, for example, Guilds of St John Fisher, St John Keble, St John Wesley and St John Bunyan. This would provide for a considerable variety, which would for a long time surprise and perhaps exasperate people who passed on their lawful occasions from a Fisher to a Bunyan parish or *vice versa*, but eventually corners would be rubbed off and toleration would increase. We cannot at present see how it is going to become possible for the lion to lie down with the lamb, but that is because we have a limited vision. There is an old promise that 'They shall not hurt nor destroy in all my holy mountain, saith the Lord.'

It is easy to make plans for other people. When the time comes to adopt them oneself, it is found that sacrifice is required. The sacrifice of principle should not be asked for, but it is in these matters of very great importance to be sure that what is called principle is really that, and nothing else. It is dangerous to allow oneself to attribute motives of arrogance to those who disagree with one or do not admit one to fellowship with them. But it is even more dangerous to the soul to take one's stand on some private mound of pride or prejudice, and persuade oneself that it is principle. Before you say, 'I cannot move from my position', be sure that you are really standing on the Rock of Ages. And, finally, it is important to bear in mind that in appreciation of the real shame and dishonour of disunion the leaders are everywhere far ahead of the rank and file.

The Anglican Communion occupies a strategic position in this matter. It has been described as a 'Bridge Church'. The title is not very accurate, as the Anglican Communion does not actually join any two Churches. But what is meant is that the Anglican Communion has affinities with the Orthodox and Roman Catholics on one side, and with non-episcopalian Reformed Churches on the other. It seems clearly desirable to keep the doors open on both sides, though there is a certain fear that the draught from a too widely-opened door on one side will cause the door on the other side to slam.

12

The Christian Outlook

THERE is no room for either optimism or pessimism. These things in any case are largely temperamental, and help little towards a true analysis of a situation. But there is a relevant thing called faith. This does not mean confidence that everything will be all right, but confidence that we are on the side of truth. No one can ever take that from us. The situation may at times be very dark. The opposition may at times be very strong, and our own forces very weak. Evidence may even drive us to the conclusion that things will be worse still before they are better. Yet, if we have the truth, we are not afraid. We go about our business, or we look in imagination round the world, and we become aware of the existence of millions of people who care nothing for our faith, and millions who deliberately and sometimes contemptuously reject it. Yet we can say to ourselves all the time, 'They do not know what I know. I know in whom I have believed.'

What enemies are there? There is, in the true sense, only one enemy, Satan, the lord of the kingdom of Sin. He is to be fought unceasingly, implacably. With him there can be no compromise, no bargain, no gentleman's agreement. His purpose is to ruin and destroy you, and you must fight against him. This book is not a sermon, but it is legitimate to say, even here, that for the purpose of carrying on this essential battle there is an armoury of grace, which has been tried and found not wanting.

The other supposed enemies are merely difficulties. It may be that Satan has something to do with it. As Christians know well from their own experience, he has a very large practice, and very ingenious methods. But the supposed enemies are human beings, men and women, and therefore in no case all bad. They constitute the territory which has to be redeemed rather than the enemy who has to be overcome.

In the next place, Christianity, moving towards the conversion of the world, meets with an enormous mass of religious indifferentism. No direct controversy with that is attempted in these pages, because those who have fallen victims to it will not be among the readers of this book.

There is, however, a very large class of persons who would acknowledge, if pressed, that they take a spiritual view of life. They are not materialists in the philosophic sense, and they are not materialists in the sense of believing that money is the only thing that matters. They do not practise the Christian religion, partly because it demands more than they are willing to give, and partly because they have an impression that it has ceased to be relevant. A view commonly encountered at Padre's Hours, during the War, was, 'That is quite interesting, and very likely true. But it all happened a long time ago, and I want something more contemporary, or, as some put it, less static.'

To meet this, it is not likely that the present volume, or, indeed, any printed matter, will achieve much. The news that the Christian Gospel is still News, i.e. a proclamation of something that has happened, something that God has done, must as a rule be carried by an audible voice. The printed word is, of course, in its place, essential. There must be reasoning and conveying of information about facts on a scale which would daunt and overtax the hearer. Even publicity has its uses: not on the principle of commercial advertisement: 'Keep your wares continually before the public', 'What they see time after time in print, they will eventually accept' – but because the public is perpetually saying, 'Why does not the Church do something?' and it is therefore worth while to publish true information. Many would still say that, even if they had been informed of what the Church had done, but some would be honest.

Yet it remains true that what is needed is a voice. Not a voice in a pulpit. That may serve a certain purpose very well, but it is a limited purpose. Only a small number are within earshot.

The voice should, if possible, be that of a person whose motives cannot be suspected. The motives of the clergy ought not really to be suspected. They are not hypocrites, and they are not – it should by this time be fairly self-evident – in the business for what they can get. But they are professionals, and, while professionals in other professions are generally trusted, professionals in religion have, with most people, a long way to go before they start level. It may be partly their own fault, but it is the fact that they 'owe' two strokes a hole at least for the first few holes, or thirty in each game of the first set. A real churchman values the clergy of his Church. If he sees weakness in them he will pray for them, and work with them. He knows that they are indispensable. And there is no relationship in the world happier or more rewarding then that of priest and people at its best. But by the public the cleric is discounted. He is not feared or hated. In fact, he is generally rather liked. But he is not taken seriously.

In France a remarkable new technique is being worked out here and there. The priest is very much part of it, but he acts, for eight hours a day, as a factory-worker, side by side with the other workers. It is known that he is a priest, and he brings religion into the factory. And the religion that he brings is not simply a gentle hint, or a cheery 'Why don't I ever see you on Sunday?' – but the Mass. By permission of the works manager and with the necessary dispensation from the ecclesiastical authorities, he says Mass in the factory at the end of the day's work. Those whose custom it already is to hear Mass on Sunday hear it, as usual, in the Parish Church. Some of those whose custom it has not hitherto been for many years to hear Mass at all, or to acknowledge any religious obligation, now hear it in the factory. This practice, which is made possible by the logic of the French people and the devotion of some of the French clergy, is having remarkable results.

It is an illustration of what can be done when contact has been established. There are other methods. But, if they are to be effective, they must follow the French lead in touching a main spring. It need not be precisely the same spring. In France *la Messe*, for good or ill, is a word to conjure with. To Churchgoers it is a duty and a privilege. Of the rest, some hate it as a relic of clerical tyranny. To others it gives a nostalgic feeling. It recalls youth, innocence and First Communion. In England, a mention of Holy Communion, which some Anglicans do in fact call the Mass, does not strike the same chord. It does not excite hatred, and though it has a vital and intimate meaning for those who habitually avail themselves of it, and though Easter pulls at the heart-strings of many a lapsed communicant, to the world at large it is just one of the things that religious people mysteriously seem to want to do.

If it could be really put to them, that this Sacrament is the cardinal example of the continuation in history of the Incarnation, God, revealed in the Holy Land in flesh and blood, God, known of us in the breaking of the bread, they might be more attentive. If they should further ever come to see that we have here the supreme case of the religious use of both Nature and Industry, the wheat, the water, and the grapes, and at the same time the livelihood of men, the way in which they earn their living and support their homes, the daily bread, now consecrated and made into holy bread, if they should ever come to find in this simple rite earth and heaven thus brought together, the attention would soon ripen into something more. And if, further, it should ever come to be their conviction that, in Richard Hooker's words, 'Christ giveth plain security that these mysteries do, as nails, fasten us to His very Cross', they might proceed to say, in the language of the same divine,

'Why should any cogitation possess the mind of a faithful communicant, but this, O my God, Thou art true; O my soul, thou art happy.'

But this is far off. It is a perpetual surprise to many who care intensely about it that people in general do not perceive either the romance, or the social significance, or the necessity, of the Christian Sacraments. It is certain that they do not. It seems to them that Holy Communion is the concern of the clergy and a few white-handed, leisured people who happen to like that kind of thing.

Nevertheless, the appeal must be to something which is recognized as central, and is big enough to carry the weight of the demand. Therefore, it seems essential, so to speak, to lead from strength. What is there that is strong enough? What is there which is behind the Sacrament and behind everything in the Christian Church?

The heart of Christianity is Christ. Christ is found by some, as has been said, chiefly in the Eucharist, by others chiefly in the four Gospels, and by others again chiefly in social reform or social revolution. Let all who will find Him where they can, and, if possible, in all these atmospheres, and many more. There are, in fact, not a few who approach through music, art, philosophy, or family or friendship. There are some who verify the truth of 'He that receiveth you, receiveth me' as Dickens' Little Em'ly did when she wrote:

When I find what you are, and what Uncle is, I think what God must be, and can cry to Him.

There are no doubt occasions and ways in which the Church does the wrong thing and should change its methods. But it must not cease to proclaim Christ. If it did, it would lose its whole *raison d'être*. That is what the Church is for. It is the Body of Christ. It should proclaim Christ as clearly as my body proclaims my presence in a room. And it must be Christ with His historic claims, 'All things have been delivered to me of the Father', and His imperious demand, 'He that will come after me, let him take up his Cross and follow me.' There has been too much sentimentalizing, too much dilution of the rich milk of the word with the water which the Modern Mind is alleged to want. That particular 'Modern Mind' which says, 'How little need we believe?' is out of date. The really contemporary mind is much more inclined to say 'What is your Christ worth? Has He something for us? Can He effect a revolution? Can He change human nature? Can He satisfy all our best and most generous instincts?' And the answer of the Church is 'Yes, He can. For He is the Saviour of mankind.'

This brings us face to face with the other claim to the allegiance of this generation, Communism. It represents, as everyone knows, one of the two modern reactions against the extreme individualism which was flagrant in the nineteenth century. There have been two forms of Totalitarianism, a system in which the state is everything and the individual nothing or almost nothing. On the surface the two police-states, Fascism and Communism, look rather alike, but there are great differences between them. Apart from the obvious fact that Fascism did not sweep away either titles or private capital, the chief differences are that in Fascism the dictatorship is permanent, while in Communism it is said to be a temporary expedient, and that Communism has a much more philanthropic social policy and a highly developed atheistic philosophy. On the other hand Communism in recent time seems unhappily to have developed tendencies that it may itself describe as missionary, but are really Imperialistic and man-eating.

One of the cardinal intellectual errors into which it is possible for Christians to fall is that of identifying Christianity with anything, except itself. If, for example, I am a Socialist, moved thereto by Christian considerations, I should be foolish to say, 'Christianity *is* Socialism'. The reason is partly that Socialism is a smaller thing than Christianity, and partly that in the course of time thought moves on, and something better than Socialism is evolved, and then there am I, tied to my outworn political creed, which I have foolishly identified with Christianity. Thus, let it not be said that Christianity *is* Communism, or that Christianity *is* anti-Communism. Still less, however, let it be said that Christianity is indifferent. Immense harm has been done by supposing that Christianity consists of practising the private personal virtues. 'These things', said Paul to Festus and Herod Agrippa, 'were not done in a corner.' And the religion which has been the fruit of those things cannot be practised in a corner.

It would be misleading to think only of Russian Communism. It would distort the view. To begin with, few people seem able to think dispassionately about Russia. They either see red, or they see Red, when they talk of it, and they seem to forget much of what they knew and believed and valued before. Besides, to look at Russia only is misleading, because Russia is ex-Tsarist, is Oriental, and has had a violent revolution, all of which things make Communist Russia very different from what a Communist Britain, or Sweden, or Holland would be.

The Communist theory of Marx arose as a protest against Capitalism. Capital was defined as greed, cruelty, oppression, and exploitation, i.e. not merely likely to produce such vices, but as consisting of them. Christianity was thought of as the ally of Capitalism. It was allowed that primitive Christianity had a certain good, revolutionary quality about it, but it had become a dope. Actually, the word 'dope' in this connexion was first used, not by Marx, but by Charles Kingsley.

For Capitalism, if it be thus defined, Christianity can have no liking. The picture of the rich man, sitting in his luxurious office, and working to bring about a war in some part of the world so that he may sell munitions to both sides, or, worse still, so that in the distress of after-war he may grow richer by manipulating the disturbed exchanges, this is clearly devilish. It is in any case dangerous that one man, or one group of men, should control enormous masses of capital.

It has, however, to be remembered that Capitalism in our own country has been a good deal ironed out in recent years, by taxation, death duties, and the development of the social services. The Communist says that all that is simply playing with the problem. That is the reason for his unpopularity with official Labour. Nothing is so exasperating as to have your principles pushed to an alleged logical conclusion which is not welcome. Remember the case of Roebuck and John Tanner in *Man and Superman*. Roebuck had always considered himself an advanced thinker, and here was Tanner accusing him of being old-fashioned and Victorian!

What is the alleged logical conclusion? It is, economically, the elimination of private capital and the establishment of the Classless State, but there is a philosophy behind it.

Instead of the present system we are to have a system in which there is taken from each according to his power and there is given to each according to his need. A man works and draws what he requires, towels, trousers, tobacco and tomato-sauce. Some of us think that it might be just tolerable to have to go to the national or international bureau for everything, but is there not something to be said for choice? If I wish to go without tobacco for a long time in order to buy the *Encyclopaedia Britannica* (in its new cosmopolitan edition) or the *Dictionary of International Biography*, or, conversely, if I wish to sell my Encyclopaedia and have one glorious dinner on the proceeds, may I not do it? There are, of course, arguments for and against these courses, but is it not a good thing that I should be able to choose? And should I be able under the system to choose freely? It is notorious that revolutions grind away many of the imponderables that make so much difference to life, but is it certain that in a non-capitalistic ordered state they would come back? There would no doubt be a Free National Theatre, but it would be controlled, and only permitted plays would be acted. There might even be cricket at Lord's, or, more probably, the Oval, but it is also possible that Denis Compton would not be allowed to score more than a hundred in a match, unless, of course, it were a Test Match against some capitalistic country.

The system seems to undermine responsibility. There is, of course, that danger even in the Social Services that we have. There are parents now who sit back, prepared to let the State do everything, forgetful of the fact that the most essential thing of all, and the one thing that the State cannot do for their children, is to give them a good father and a good mother.

The small capitalist is not historically a very attractive figure. The peasant who becomes a little richer than the other peasants may turn into the village money-lender, exploiting his poor neighbours. But it is not altogether a pity that the Savings Movement has made the British a nation of small capitalists. Three hundred pounds in the Savings Bank gives stability to a man's life. The peasant who owns land is a stronger person than the landless hireling, and much stronger than the serf.

The other plank in the platform is the classless society. Is that really possible? It does not exist in Russia. There are classes there, though not the same classes as there were. It is said to be provisional. As soon as the time is ripe, dictatorship and the provisional class-system will be abolished, and history will begin. It is difficult not to be sceptical about this, because men are very hardly brought to relinquish power, except at the bidding of some other-worldly motive, which in this case is not forthcoming.

Anyhow, is it a thing to aim at? Elimination of the idle rich? Yes. And of the idle poor? Yes. The extremes were terrifying. But is there no interest in variety? Snobbery is, of course, foolish, but is there nothing in what is called 'good family'? The House of Lords has its uses. There are points of view from which it is a pity that all the great country houses are doomed. Is the English 'great lady' worth preserving? She is picturesque, and may be very useful, but she is expensive. She requires a background. Yet it is not certain that her total abolition would be a total gain. In fact, the break-up of big estates has often had the effect of turning what used to be semi-public property, open to the public, into privately owned small properties, from which the public are excluded.

Consider other cases. The college student is protected. He is delivered from the necessity of earning his living in the market, because it is believed that he will be useful in the future. The learned Professor, who lives in an ancient College and has spacious rooms and a servant, is protected, because he produces the goods.

Are they tainted goods? The academic mind is very sensitive about this. To-day, when education is more and more helped, or entirely provided, by the State, some educators think that the battle for intellectual freedom has been lost, and all that they can now do is to register the decisions of a Ministry. This is no doubt an exaggeration, but there are dangers to intellectual freedom. In America the rich benefactor has been known to wish to control the kind of economics that is taught in his University. In Nazi Germany the professorial chairs were controlled by the State. The present writer at a Conference in 1937 in Berlin, which was intended to conciliate British opinion, heard some very disquieting admissions made by German Professors. In Russia it seems that there are to-day the beginnings of a politically orthodox biology, which is to the academic, truth-loving mind a terrible thing. All this is very alarming. At present it looks in England as if the teaching profession would be strong enough to stand for teaching according to conscience, but pressure might increase.

This leads to the Communist attitude towards religion. It is essentially anti-Christian, anti-God : sometimes in rather a simple, unsophisticated way, as when Yaroslavsky writes that:

The correct explanation of the origin of hail, rain, drought, the appearance of insect plagues, the properties of various soils, and the actions of fertilizers, is the best anti-religious propaganda, and the whole of the Russian anti-God propaganda was at first very crude.

With militant atheism of this kind it would seem that Christianity has nothing or almost nothing in common. Yet, remember Shelley. He attacked God as a tyrant. His Prometheus was the great rebel against God. Yet some now feel that Shelley was only fighting against a false conception, and that he was in his queer way a preacher of the true God.

The parallel is not complete. It is notoriously difficult to judge the present situation, but the case of Communism does seem different. Shelley's world was more spiritual than that of Karl Marx. In Marx we have a deliberate republication of the first two of Hegel's dialectic propositions:

> All organic process is dialectical.
> Reality is an organic process.

together with a repudiation of Hegel's third proposition:

> Reality is idea.

Dialectic means that there is first of all a thesis, then an opposed antithesis, and then an inevitable synthesis. The word 'inevitable' is emphasized. Mechanistic materialism is abomination to Marxists. There is no coherence in it. Dialectical materialism means a belief that the cosmic process is like that. That is all that there is, and if you co-operate with that, you are on the right side, the only side. That is why Communism is a religion, and arouses fervour. The historical process is infallible. They know all the answers, not because they are conceited, but because reality is like that, and they are co-operating with the true process. That is why there is only one set of candidates at an election. It is not Freedom. But it is Communism.

It is, however, a purely mundane historical process. Within its limits (which are alleged to be the limits of reality) great progress can be, and has been, made. But there is and can be no appeal to any transcendent moral law, to the will of God. There is no such thing. There is only the historical process. Hence lying, cruelty, etc., are defended, if they are necessary in the interests of Communist theory. Expediency is the standard, and there cannot be, on orthodox Marxist grounds, any real personal initiative. The system is totalitarian and thoroughly institutional. That is why it will not last as Christianity has lasted and will last. It has not depth enough. It is self-nurtured. It will presently exhaust itself. It is institutional and nothing more.

The Communist answer to the objection that all are being bound into the same pattern is 'We want to be.' That would seem to be true of members of the Party, the only persons who are allowed to count. It is, however, always conceivable that some will not want to be, and for them, and for the willing, in case they should forget, or relax their willingness, the State is a police-state, with Siberian labour camps ready to swallow up the unorthodox.

They say sometimes, 'But Christianity also wishes to bind men into the same model.' It is false. There is no extant exact picture of the world as Christians desire to see it. The ideal situation, which Christians call the Kingdom of God, a condition in which God is really King, and is obeyed, will not come to pass without the co-operation of millions of people, most of whom have not yet begun to co-operate, many of whom do not even know that they are expected to do so. No one can say exactly what it will be like, but the principle of it is that Christ contains in Himself the ideal for every man, and that every man is capable of filling a niche in the temple. The niches are all different. And the man needs not to be bound into a predetermined order, but to be set free from his lower self, from sin, in order that he may become whatever in the providence of God he may be capable of becoming. This, and this alone, is freedom. Freedom is the thing which mankind, at this moment, most of all needs, the only way of making the best use of all the material that is available. Christianity is Freedom's best friend.

Nevertheless, let us be sure that we are standing on the true ground. Communism is strong, thorough-going and in its limited way philanthropic, and it has the fervour of a religion. Ordinary political convictions, Liberal, Conservative, or Labour, are not strong enough to stand against it. What is required is a wholly different view of life, life seen as God's creation, and as moving towards the completion of the Body of Christ. Conventional Christianity is not strong enough. The only thing which is strong enough to stand, not precisely against Communism, but above it, and all round it, and eventually on all the ground which it occupies, and much more besides, is real Christianity, a Christianity which satisfies both in theory and in practice.

Theory and practice. One of the things which Communists condemn in Christianity is its idealism. By this they seem to mean a kind of dualism, or division of life into two separated compartments, religious and secular. It appears to them that Christians are absorbed in the contemplation of celestial will-o'-the-wisps and in the performance of the duties of religion, and that they neglect earthly duties. Regarded as a description of Western Christendom in general, this is surprising indeed. We have not, as a rule, been found excessively idealist in this sense and to this extent. And, indeed, in view of the complaint, it is curious to hear that 'a new heresy, "Praktizismus" has been discovered and denounced in Eastern Germany. It consists in paying too much attention to the job in hand and not enough to Communist ideology.[1]' It seems that the dictators would like their subjects to be more 'idealist'.

The weakness, where it really exists, as it certainly does, is due not to Christian theology, but to the Fall of Man. It is not an easy thing for anyone to carry his religion right through into every action of his life, and sometimes the duty is avoided by making a cut between religion and life. It must be admitted that some of us, having no authority from Christ, or from the Church, do something like this. And this particular complaint is so commonly made that we seem driven to conclude that there must be some evidence for it.

1. D. W. Brogan in *The Spectator*, 21 January 1950.

Unverified complaints and charges are constantly passed from mouth to mouth, but there is generally some foundation for them somewhere. Yet there ought not to be. Dualism is a word which has been used in various senses, but it almost always represents a thing which Christianity should and does reject. Dualism of this kind is quite certainly to be rejected. There are traces of it at times in Christian history, and it exists to-day, but it has no warrant from the four Gospels.

Miss Evelyn Underhill, a leading authority on Mysticism, quotes in *The Mystic Way* an eloquent passage from one of the Greek Fathers about the contemplation of the Divine Nature, 'God as He is in His Limitless Splendour and Incomparable Glory', and adds that the subsequent development of this mode of thought led in some of the Greek mystical writers to 'an imperfectly Christianized version of the exclusively transcendentalist and largely impersonal mysticism of the Pagan Neoplatonists.' In contrast with that she sets 'the secret of Jesus', which she in point of fact describes, in a perfectly good and true sense, as 'a dual consciousness of reality'. She continues:

The secret of Jesus, His power as the perfect expression of completed human nature, had lain in His steady alternation of action and contemplation, the interweaving of two orders of Reality; His discovery of the 'Kingdom' in the common things of life, His ecstatic fruition of God and unwearied service of man.

Here is a consciousness, dual indeed in that it covers the whole of life, but with no dualism in the sense of dismissing secular things as either unconnected with religion or as unworthy of consideration.

The same thought is put in other language by Sir Richard Acland, M.P.:

We concede to our opponents the fantastic idea that God's action in history is limited to the insinuation of a few moral ideas into hell's own material situation. Nothing of the kind. God is every bit as much concerned with the discovery of the stirrup and the development of the conveyor-belt as in the loftiest sermons and the most intricate theological speculation.

Or, as it has been put in an even shorter way, 'As if God were interested in Mattins but not in the market, in Evensong but not in the election.'

It could almost be put in one single word – Freedom. Real Christianity believes in complete freedom for everyone, a freedom for everyone to take his place in a free society, a freedom which brings the utmost possible happiness to everyone, on the single condition that his happiness shall not mean the unhappiness of others, and moreover, freedom to choose whether he will do this or that. There must be no compulsion, not even any social pressure. If I could convert a man to my way of thinking by pressing a button in his waistcoat, I ought not to do it.

And at the back of it there is the conviction that the ideal – the word is deliberately used – for everyone is Christ. In this conception of freedom there is no limitation, no political or economic *arrière pensée*, no wish to bend to a prescribed pattern. It is a conception which, where it exists or any approximation to it exists, gives a contemporary meaning to an old saying, 'With men it is impossible, but not with God. With God all things are possible.'

> Make me a captive, Lord,
> And then I shall be free.

It is perfectly true that there is in the vocabulary of Christ an imperative – 'I say unto you.' And sometimes the alternative indicated is very severe. But it does not run on the material plane. And it is not a threat. The condemnation of hypocrites is the devastating but very quiet verdict, 'They have their reward.' And always man is free to choose whether or not he will be a disciple. The instruments of grace are very powerful, stronger than the hammer of Thor or the hammer of totalitarian coercion, but they are held in such careful, loving hands that they will not crack the egg-

1. *Nothing Left to Believe*, 92.

shell of a single conscience. 'When the Son of Man cometh, will he find faith on the earth?' No one can say. It depends on the answer given by the sons of men. That answer must be the free expression of their personal will. Nevertheless, the desire of the Son of Man is, 'I will that, where I am, they also may be with me.'

*The following pages
describe other recent and
relevant Pelicans and
Penguin Classics*

Comparative Religion

BY A. C. BOUQUET

A 89

In presenting this panorama of the great
religions of the world the author has striven,
he says, 'to write as a scientist, not an advocate'. In recent years there have been remarkable advances in the study of comparative religion, and much of this new material
is passed on to the general reader for the first
time in this authoritative survey. Its theme
is the religious quest of mankind, as manifested in many distinctive faiths, and in his
analysis of these Dr Bouquet examines the
reasons why they have maintained – or lost –
their significance, and what are their prospects of survival in the rapidly-changing
modern world. The religions of India and
the Far East are given particular consideration in this study, which *The Times Educational Supplement* has described as 'an abbre-
viated encyclopaedia of religions'. Written
expressly as a Pelican, and first published
in 1942, it has now been re-issued many
times. (2s 6d)

The Four Gospels

One of the most important books to appear under the Penguin imprint recently is Dr E. V. Rieu's translation of THE FOUR GOSPELS. With this, the fourth of his own works in the series of which he is general editor, Dr Rieu has discharged another monumental task to rival his earlier single-handed translation of Homer. He has treated this fourfold account of the greatest story in the world primarily as a work of literature, and it is as such that it takes a rightful place among the Penguin Classics. But the publication of a new version of the Gospels is much more than a literary event. It is an invitation to look again at the reported speech of Christ, at words and events that have influenced so many entire generations and perhaps grown over-familiar to some in another form. This translation is based for the most part on the fourth-century Codex Sinaiticus, the oldest of the ancient Greek manuscripts extant. It is introduced by a long and extremely interesting essay, in which the translator compares with the original the beautiful Elizabethan English of the Authorized Version, explains his reasons for making this new attempt, and reveals some of the difficulties and something of the interest and excitement that his study has brought him. It is decorated with wood-engravings by Reynolds Stone, who has designed a headpiece for each Gospel. (Paper-covered 2s 6d, and cloth-bound 7s 6d)

*

Other Classics

After the Bible itself probably the best-known and best-loved book in Christendom is THE IMITATION OF CHRIST, Thomas à Kempis's guide towards Christian perfection, which for over five hundred years has continued to exercise a widespread influence over Christians of every age and race. Unfortunately most English translators have tended to misrepresent this book – either by making unacknowledged alterations in the text to accord with their personal views, or by presenting it in a pseudo-Jacobean style. Thus many would-be readers have passed it by, and missed the advantage of Thomas's profound wisdom, his clarity of thought and vision, his wide knowledge of the Scriptures and Fathers, and his clear understanding of human nature and its needs. It was time for a new translation, and L. Sherley-Price, a senior Chaplain of the Royal Navy, has provided it for the Penguin Classics series. His, the first unabridged edition in modern English, presents a complete, accurate, and readable version to the public. (2s 6d)

*

Dorothy L. Sayers has translated THE INFERNO, the first part of Dante's DIVINE COMEDY, for the Penguin Classics series; and no previous translator has succeeded in following as closely as she does not only the metre and rhyme of the original, but the subtle variations of rhythm by which Dante expresses his changing moods. The press comments which greeted its publication were outstanding. *John o' London's* called it 'a landmark in English publishing', and *Time and Tide* said 'of all verse translations of this poem into English, Miss Sayers' appears to me to be the most readable'. Sir Ronald Storrs wrote in *The Observer*: 'Encouraged by her almost loving guidance to a first careful reading of this Penguin, the proselyte will remain profoundly in her debt for a life-enhancing pilgrimage of the spirit through the most tremendous poem in the world'; and Sir Adrian Boult singled it out in the 'Books of the Year' column of *The Sunday Times*, commenting: 'I must say that I have had the most enormous pleasure from Miss Sayers' introduction to her Penguin *Dante*. It seems to me to combine a remarkable scholarship with an irresistible delight in the work in hand, which makes anyone who reads one page of it long to get down to reading the whole comedy again.' (2s 6d)

*

The monks of the Middle Ages did not always occupy their leisure hours religiously. Sometimes they wrote poems – to a season, a mood, an event or, more often, to a lady. Another Penguin Classic, MEDIAEVAL LATIN LYRICS,* is a collection of these and other exquisite verses of the period in a modern English version by Helen Waddell, who is a well known and accomplished translator from the French, Latin, and Chinese. 'For most of us,' wrote *Country Life* when the book first appeared, 'the thousand years from 200 to 1200 represent an arid, lifeless waste. Miss Waddell's books are an open sesame to the life that was in them. That life shows itself as lusty, outrageous, and lovable as ever appetized and agonized the Greece of Pericles or Caesar's Rome.' (3s)

Not available for U.S.A.

The Life of Jesus

*

Two very different Penguin publications are concerned with the life of Jesus. The first is a Pelican, THE LIFE OF JESUS (1s 6d) (A 189) by C. J. Cadoux, a survey of what in fact we know about Jesus the Man from the historical evidence available. Loyalty to this evidence, in the author's view, demands a frank recognition of the human limitations within which Christ's life on earth was lived; and theological statements must not be allowed to stand in place of the historical record, however much they may be needed to draw out its ultimate implications. *The Fortnightly Review* commented: 'This volume can be commended with confidence to all who wish to know what manner of man Jesus was, what He did, and what He taught.' The second book is George Moore's famous novel THE BROOK KERITH* (Penguin 844, 2s 6d), which is based on a supposition that Jesus did not die on the Cross. According to the story He was rescued by Joseph of Arimathea, and returned to a humble life of toil and meditation among the Essenes, a strict religious community who lived beside the Brook Kerith. He was working there as a shepherd, having renounced his Messianic claim, when St Paul met him many years later. The story is a beautiful and reverent work of the imagination, and in no sense a perverse piece of religious controversy which might anger or offend those who accept the Bible story of the life and death of Christ.

* *Not available for U.S.A.*

The English Middle Classes*

ANGUS MAUDE AND ROY LEWIS

A 263

A critical survey of the history, present conditions, and prospects of
the middle classes, from whom come most of the nation's brains,
leadership, and organizing ability. Professor Trevelyan wrote in
The Observer: 'It will help everyone to think more clearly and to
realize the nature of our situation.' (2s 6d)

England in Transition

DOROTHY GEORGE

A 248

England as it appeared to Defoe, discussing the situation immediately prior to the dawn of the Machine Age – the coming of indus-
trialism, the village in transition – showing how some of the evils
often supposed to be due to the Industrial Revolution were also
present in the 'golden age'. (2s)

A Forgotten Kingdom

SIR LEONARD WOOLLEY

A 261

The results of recent excavations in the Turkish Hatay which throw
new light on the great pre-classical empires of Sumer, Babylon, and
Egypt, on the art of Minoan Crete, the Bronze Age culture of
Cyprus, and the trade and economics of Greece. (2s 6d)

* *Not available for U.S.A.*

THE PELICAN HISTORY OF ENGLAND

❋

While each volume is complete in itself, this whole series has been planned to provide an intelligent and consecutive guide to the development of English society in all its aspects. Of the eight volumes, seven are already available:

THE BEGINNINGS OF ENGLISH SOCIETY (from the Anglo-Saxon Invasion)
Dorothy Whitelock, Fellow of St Hilda's College, Oxford

ENGLISH SOCIETY IN THE EARLY MIDDLE AGES
Doris Mary Stenton, Lecturer at Reading University

ENGLAND IN THE LATE MIDDLE AGES
A. R. Myers, Lecturer at Liverpool University

TUDOR ENGLAND
S. T. Bindoff, Professor of History at Queen Mary College, London

ENGLAND IN THE SEVENTEENTH CENTURY
Maurice Ashley, M.A.

ENGLAND IN THE EIGHTEENTH CENTURY
J. H. Plumb, Fellow of Christ's College, Cambridge

ENGLAND IN THE NINETEENTH CENTURY
David Thomson, Fellow of Sidney Sussex College, Cambridge

The remaining volume, which will follow as soon as possible, is:

ROMAN BRITAIN
Professor Ian Richmond, King's College, Newcastle-on-Tyne

An Introduction to the Bible

STANLEY COOK

A 144

The intention of this volume, specially written as a Pelican, and now in its second large
impression, is to survey the nature and the
history of the Bible. Its author, Dr Stanley
Cook, who was Regius Professor of Hebrew
at Cambridge, and a distinguished authority
on Comparative Religion, traces the origins
of the many and diverse books which are
assembled in the Bible, compares them with
other sacred writings and analyses the fundamental ideas which have caused the Bible
to be regarded as a unified whole. In two
chapters of particular interest he outlines the
methods of approach and study most likely
to give the general reader an enlightened
understanding of a book so often taken for
granted, or accepted uncritically, as a body
of doctrine.

Dr Cook wrote not only as a scholar and
historian, but also as an avowed and convinced Christian, and in this scrutiny of the
composition and meaning of the Bible he re-
states the reasons why the Bible is to be regarded as the basis of the Christian faith. (2s)